# COMING
## OF AGE

**OUR JOURNEY INTO ADULTHOOD**

# CATE LESOURD

**OAKDALE**
PUBLISHING GROUP

Published by Oakdale Publishing Group LLC
18462 Lincoln Road, Purcellville, VA 20132, USA
www.oakdalepublishinggroup.com

ISBN: 978-1-7377668-0-3 (paperback)
ISBN: 978-1-7377668-1-0 (ebook)

Cover art by Becca Strasburg
Author photo by Rob Tracy
Art and design direction by Larry Taylor
Interior design by Ragont Design
Ebook production by BB eBooks

Printed in the United States of America

I dedicate this book to you.

May it be an encouragement in your own journey.

# CONTENTS

# INTRODUCTION

O ur transition from college to adulthood is filled with challenges, disappointments, and a lot of uncertainty. The fears and anxiety can feel crippling at times. We hesitate to share what is going on beneath the surface, so we feel isolated in our own experiences and emotions. If we take our cue from social media, we will have a flawed measure of comparison and a false view of reality.

Most books about our twenties are written from the perspective of psychologists, business leaders, and experts on how to live through those years. While helpful, it is rare to hear the voices of those who are in the midst of the transition.

I wrote this book because I often felt alone in my circumstances and overwhelmed with the uncertainties of my life, especially those related to my career. I want to tell my story because I do not want anyone to live in isolation, fear, or anxiety during this unique time in our lives. Our twenties are filled with periods of doubt and uncertainty. It is time for us to talk about them. It is time for this book.

My story, of course, is only one story. Over the course of several years, I sent out two questionnaires to over a thousand young adults across the nation ranging from college seniors to those in their early thirties. The first questionnaire focused on the initial adjustment from college, and the second questionnaire targeted the relationships and career changes that continue to evolve throughout your twenties and early thirties. Overall, the questions asked respondents to reflect on their own journey and provided an opportunity to share their difficulties and personal growth.

In reviewing hundreds of responses, I was most surprised by the depth and honesty of the answers. People *wanted* to talk about their struggles and challenges. For some, it was the first time anyone had intentionally asked about them. For others, it was their first opportunity to express their own thoughts and share their own stories.

This book discusses the major themes of the adjustment into adulthood from the perspectives of those who are currently living it. In addition to sharing aspects of my own life, I share quotes from the survey respondents to highlight the experiences, emotions, and thoughts that commonly occur during the post-grad years. Names, locations, and other identifying information were changed, unless otherwise approved, to protect the individuals who were willing to share in this book. I am deeply grateful for the openness of so many twenty- and thirty-somethings who shared their raw experiences with me. This book is far more complete with their voices.

As you read, I am eager for you to see purpose in your own story as it unfolds and take courage as you navigate this unique journey into adulthood.

# PART ONE

# ADJUSTING TO THE ADULT WORLD

## CHAPTER 1

# GREAT EXPECTATIONS

"Courage, dear heart."

C. S. LEWIS

I began my senior year of college with no idea what I wanted to do after graduation. I sometimes joked that I wished I could major in minors. My generalist nature was evident by my choice of academic courses. Throughout four years, I took a variety of classes and built relationships with professors from three entirely different fields of study: communications, human services, and entrepreneurship.

This breadth of experience contributed to the complexity of considerations for my post-grad plans, which ranged from applying for a year-long service fellowship in Africa to moving to Nashville without a job. Due to deadlines, I focused on fellowships and programs first. The delay was fortunate because I did not know specifically what kind of job I wanted.

Over the winter holiday break, I learned of a national competition at a large public relations agency. The prompt was to create an idea for a post-grad summer adventure to help experience the world beyond the cubicle. The winning candidate would secure a company-sponsored summer experience *and* a full-time job afterwards. I thought to myself, *Can this be real?* Then I looked at the deadline. It was due *that day.*

Immediately, I set to work. The competition limited candidates to stay within the fifty states, so I thought, *Why not travel to every single one of them?* With a campaign called #50stateswithcate, I planned to highlight the best views, sites, and aspects of major cities across the United States.

As I celebrated New Year's Eve that evening, I joked with my friends how unbelievable the opportunity would be, not thinking it could ever happen. When I failed to receive any confirmation of my submission, the competition quickly slipped my mind.

A few weeks later, however, the company called, saying they loved my idea. They wanted me to move forward to the next round of the competition: create a video pitch. I had taken a few video courses in college, so I worked to show visually and creatively what my campaign would entail. Despite my computer crashing forcing me to learn new software, I submitted my video right before the deadline.

Within days, I received a phone call. The company was impressed with my video and told me I had moved on to the next round as one of six semifinalists. Employees across the company's American offices would vote on their favorite video to choose the finalists.

When my university found out that I and a fellow student—a friend of mine—were both semifinalists in this national competition, the communications department wrote an article about us that circled around on social media.

The buzz began. Students mentioned it to me in class. Professors emailed me about it. Friends posted on social media that they were cheering me on. I even heard from people back home in Virginia, friends in Nashville, and family members across the country. Friends studying abroad contacted me. All of a sudden, my entire social network seemed to be aware of the competition. Then I learned I was one of the three finalists and would be flown to Chicago for a day of in-person interviews. My university posted a follow-up article. The student magazine interviewed me for its cover story. While I was humbled and grateful for all the exposure and affirmation, I also felt overwhelmed.

Friends' opinions ranged from, "You can't turn down an opportunity like this" to "What about Nashville? Didn't you want to move there?" From no plan at all, my life was quickly unfolding in favor of this potential opportunity.

I flew to Chicago on February 23, one of the coldest days of the year. I experienced the city for the first time in its true form—at 7° with wind chills of 20 to 30 below. *If I like the city in the dead of winter,* I thought, *surely I would like it even more in the summer.*

Following a tour of the office, we three finalists rotated through group interviews, including a one-on-one with the CEO. Afterward, we were split up and tasked with a creative challenge, accompanied by our own personal videographer to capture our experience. Once we completed the challenge, we returned to the office and drew straws for the amount of prep time we would have to create a presentation.

I drew the short straw. After thirty minutes of pulling together a presentation, I walked into the conference room and presented to a room full of the company's top executives. While I wished I could have had more time, I knew I had tried my best.

After a social hour with employees, the three of us shared a taxi back to O'Hare Airport. The entire trip had been a whirlwind, and I left eager and hopeful to win the competition.

Back on campus, I shared the unforgettable interview experience with close friends. The following week, the university magazine appeared with me on the front cover and a four-page article spread with images from the earlier photo shoot. Friends texted me photos and shared the article on social media.

The magazine staff did a wonderful job on the cover story, but inevitably I felt pressure to live up to the expectations since everyone in my social circles knew about this potential job opportunity. My fears were realized when, the very next day, the company informed me in a phone call that I was *not* the winner.

Rejection: We all know that gut-wrenching feeling. I'd had such hopes, and to end up so close to winning was a major disappointment. And while it crushed me to lose, the news was slightly offset by an offer for a post-graduate summer internship with the agency.

As I processed the results with close friends and family, I felt compelled to share the news more broadly, especially since everyone was curious about the results. Unlike many of my classmates announcing their job acceptances, I was announcing a job rejection. I felt it was important. "Why am I sharing this on Facebook? We tend to only post positive life events, and I felt like because this potential job opportunity gathered so much publicity (even with the recent magazine article), I wanted to be able to authentically share the moments that we all face: rejection, disappointment, and hurt."

While most people are not the face of a national competition, there are countless individuals who apply for fellowships, graduate programs, or jobs and are rejected. We don't typically promote or willingly share those realities, so it is easy to feel alone in our rejections or disappointments. Yet when it seems everyone else is sailing through their lives, we need to remember that to get a desired yes, we often have to deal with many discouraging and frustrating nos.

It is important to deal with the reality of disappointment. In times of rejection, it helps to give ourselves time and space to process it. When we identify our emotions and work through the disappointment or anxiety, we can move forward toward what could be next.

## CONTINUED UNCERTAINTY

After accepting the fact that I had lost the competition, I considered the internship offer. A key factor in the decision related to the location. Chicago was not on my radar at all. If you had asked me before the competition, my guess was that I would move to Nashville after I graduated.

Why Nashville? I had spent a summer interning at a company the year before and had fallen in love with the city. In that time, I had developed meaningful friendships that would act as a foundation of community in Nashville. Even though I did not have a job lined up at that point, I felt confident the professional connections would help me integrate into the city.

Conversely, I had no prior connection to Chicago, so it would be an entirely new experience. Moving to Chicago, however, would provide an opportunity to live in a large city, which I had not experienced before.

If we view a decision as only what could be right and wrong, we imply that if we choose anything but the right option, the outcome will be wrong. That places a burden on us as decision makers. When I viewed my own choice as deciding between what was right and wrong for my life, I felt stress over the options, angst about the decision, and fear of the unknown. While it is important to be intentional about decisions and the potential consequences or results, I realized I did not need to add extra pressure or expectations on myself as it related to this one decision.

As I thought about it, I saw two good options—and one did not foreclose the other. Moving to Nashville after graduation would be less of a risk since I had already enjoyed living there for several months. But still, if I moved to Chicago after graduation and did not like the city, I knew I could always move to Nashville.

Realizing that my decision was not irreversible, I felt the freedom to choose Chicago, the lesser-known option. I moved to a city I had been in for a total of thirty hours, not knowing whether I would enjoy it there or whether an internship would result in a full-time job offer.

15

My post-grad story began with saying yes to more uncertainty. At the time I made my post-grad plans, I said yes to Chicago because it was a risk I was willing to take.

Graduation day came and went on May 23rd. I packed up the life I had known at college and entered the unknown world of post-grad life. On June 7, I flew to Chicago from Washington, D.C. and was picked up by a friend at the airport. For my first week in the city, I crashed on the couch of two friends—my only friends in Chicago at the time—as I waited for an apartment to become available. Not knowing how long I would stay in Chicago, I had decided to sublet an apartment for the summer before committing to a full-year lease.

On June 8, I started the post-graduate internship program. During the first day, I met the cohort of about twenty other twentysomethings, received a mentor at the company, and was assigned client projects for the summer. My first adult job had begun.

Working at a large PR agency quickly became a meaningful and fun experience as my first job after college. Employees had a ping-pong table and unlimited supply of LaCroix in the kitchen, but more important, we worked for notable clients alongside creative people. Even though we were at the bottom of the career ladder, we were in a prime position to learn and have hands-on experiences with other professionals. I quickly developed relationships with fellow interns as well as others within the agency. From company-wide service days to ongoing weekly happy hours, I knew I was fortunate to work at a company that cared so much about its culture.

Each week, agency leadership hosted a lunch-and-learn for the intern class to learn more about the company and the PR industry. For a fresh college graduate, this focused attention and mentorship helped make the transition into the working world more seamless.

During the second half of the summer, we were split into two teams and given a prompt to create a PR campaign. In addition to the client work throughout the week, we worked on the campaign together after work hours. As the summer internship came to a close, we presented our campaign to the agency.

Throughout the time on this group project, we all interviewed for the eight open full-time positions. Although I knew there was a possibility I would not be offered a job, I had to decide if I would stay in Chicago whether or not I had a job offer. By this time, I had spent a summer in the city and fallen in love with Chicago. I decided I wanted to stay in Chicago, even if it meant delaying a full-time job again. When I prepared for my interview at the end of my internship, I also looked for an apartment. I signed a lease before I knew about the status of the job offer.

Thankfully, after days of waiting, I accepted a full-time position at the same agency. The wait was over. My career had officially begun.

## NEW BEGINNINGS

It was a beautiful, sunny day in Chicago the following April as I commuted downtown on the train. I arrived at my desk and chatted with a few coworkers about our weekends. Checking my email, I began a quick assignment for a colleague.

An instant message from an executive popped up asking me to chat for a moment. Earlier that month, she had asked me about my calendar availability because she wanted to meet about an upcoming project. I assumed the meeting was to discuss that work, so I picked up my notebook and walked toward her desk. Before I could even say hello, she told me we should go for a walk.

We moved toward a nearby conference room, which was near the Human Resources and Finance departments. Conference rooms were hard to come by at the agency, so I did not think much about it. I walked into the room first and as I sat down, I saw the head of HR walking behind me. My heart sank.

The executive with whom I had worked closely did not say a word; she was quiet with a sad expression on her face. The head of HR quickly explained there had been some recent changes in clients. The resulting financial impacts affected me.

"Your position has been eliminated."

No one can ever prepare you to hear those words. I burst into tears as the head of HR continued.

"And today is your last day. We recommend that you leave immediately."

Those words hit me the hardest. My mind raced to my coworkers and how I would not get to say thank you and goodbye or have any sort of closure with the relationships I had built over the last year. I thought about my teams and how they would have to pick up my assignments with no notice. I felt responsible for my work and realized that I would not finish the assignments I had been working on that morning.

The rest of the meeting was a blur—something about my last paycheck, packing up my things, and how I was not the only one affected. They asked if I wanted to leave from the side door, but I said I would pick up my bag first.

They left me in the room and gave me a few moments to regain my composure before heading out. I knew crying in a conference room would not help, so I took a few deep breaths and stood up. In a haze, I walked toward my desk. I barely remember moving—it felt like a true out-of-body experience.

A mentor sat across from my desk, and I remember being concerned over what she would say if she saw my facial expression and watery eyes. But as I walked back toward my desk, I noticed she was in the middle of a meeting in another conference room. I did not get the chance to say goodbye.

Trying to be discreet, I closed my half-open computer, only to find it had already been logged out by the company. HR had said they would pack up my things, so I took one final look at my desk, picked up my bag, and walked out the door.

As I stood in the elevator bay next to the kitchen, I remembered an unopened package of hummus I had put in the refrigerator that morning. I walked toward the kitchen to grab it because that was three dollars that I now needed (the things that go through your mind when you are in shock). But when I tapped my badge against the electronic lock on the kitchen door, I discovered it was deactivated. I was already locked out. It was if I had never worked there.

I rode the elevator down to the lobby and walked through the foyer. Then I sat outside the building and called my parents to tell them the news. There I was: twenty-three years old, sitting on a stone bench, crying to my parents after losing my first job.

Minutes later, a few of my coworkers from my cohort came down and cried with me. They were just as shocked as I was. At that point, they had heard other colleagues were affected, so everyone felt a sense of fear and uncertainty. After a few minutes, they had to go back to work. I said goodbye, then watched them turn around and walk back into the office building.

Still in shock, I walked around the city and talked with a few college friends on the phone. I told my church small group and immediately received encouragement. That night, a group of my coworkers and I gathered to eat dinner together as we all processed the emotional events of the day. I was the only one from my cohort laid off that day.

My sudden layoff was a shocking and traumatic experience. I could never have prepared to lose my job in a matter of seconds. I could never have known I would be laid off about a year after graduating college. I could never have expected to have a major life crisis happen at twenty-three years old.

My life had changed instantly. Within minutes, I had been told my position was eliminated and to leave immediately. Within minutes, I had walked out without the opportunity to say proper goodbyes to any of my colleagues. Within minutes, I was out of a job, salary, and health benefits.

A day that had begun as any other day had left me unemployed and uncertain about what the next day held.

I also battled a sense of embarrassment. I had prided myself on checking all the boxes of becoming independent out of college. I accepted a job offer. I received healthcare benefits. I moved to a new city. I rented an apartment. I was paying off my student loans. Now, almost all of those decisions were forced to a halt or reversed.

Even though I was told that the layoff was not due to my performance, and even though I learned there were a number of people laid off that morning, I felt shame and fear that I had done something wrong. I could not help but wonder, *Why is this happening to me?* In light of how much time, money, and effort the company had invested into recruiting me to work at that agency, I was in utter disbelief that the company had decided to let me go a year later.

On the personal side, as someone who highly valued my interpersonal relationships, I felt a deep sense of pain knowing I would not have any sort of closure with my coworkers and teams. No goodbye happy hour. No email announcement. Nothing.

I applied for unemployment benefits and suspended my student loans. I sat on my bed crying, overwhelmed at the realities I now faced. As I started making financial decisions, I was afraid for my future and felt discouraged at being forced into survival mode. My life had taken an unexpected turn, and I was concerned how it would affect my career trajectory.

My mind loves to bridge connections and ideas, so I often try to understand or add meaning as to why situations unfold the way they do. Yet whenever I tried to make sense of what was happening, the thoughts would send me into a negative downward spiral.

I needed to accept the truth that I will not understand many trials and situations in life.

With a layoff, you are simply on the cut list of names. It is not personal; it's just business. But it sure feels personal when it affects your life so personally. Even if the decision is not tied to our performance, we cannot help but feel worthless and doubt the value we bring to a company when we are thrown out at the first sign of financial trouble.

The day after I was laid off, I wrote a blog post that I shared with my social network. As my passion for speaking about difficult topics was increasing, I decided to share what happened. I was deeply moved by the friends and family who reached out to me during that time. While I do not wish that experience on anyone, I am grateful for the ways sharing my story led to encouraging words from friends and family across the country. Friends reached out to me about their own layoff experiences, which was a needed reminder that I was not alone.

Like anyone in a time of loss, I had a long, nonlinear process of grieving ahead of me.

## GRIEF, INSECURITY, AND IDENTITY

It was hard enough job searching in college. Being unemployed as an adult felt like a different pressure. Since I was already living on my own and responsible for bills, I needed to find a new job as soon as possible. I expected the job search to be easier compared to when I was a student. I was now a college graduate with a year at a large PR agency under my belt. Since most entry-level jobs required experience, I initially felt hopeful I would find something quickly.

Weeks went by, then months. I heard nothing but silence from applications. I felt increasingly more discouraged, embarrassed, and a bit hopeless. Contrary to what I had thought, it seemed as though it had been easier to find a job fresh out of college or as an intern than it was after a year of professional experience. It felt as if my entire first year of working in the professional world meant nothing. I did not fully understand the truth of the phrase—"It's easier to find a job when you have one"—until my season of unemployment. The pressure mounted to find *something*.

Naturally, friends would ask if I had heard anything. No. Was I not doing enough? And I felt judged, mostly due to my own insecurities and my own perceptions of others. I now recognize I cared too much what other people thought about me and my job search. But at the time, I felt very fragile emotionally and wrestled with insecurities of my worth and abilities. Especially because my Chicago community was limited at the time, I wished my newer friends could have seen the success I'd had in college. I did not want them to think of me as a failure. I felt a need to prove to others—and myself—that I was hirable, talented, and intelligent. I was building my sense of community and establishing my place in Chicago with a shattered view of myself.

Since I was still trying to make friends, I remember attending events and gatherings and dreading the inevitable, "So tell us your name, where you're from, and what you do." You do not realize how much you value your occupation until you have none to talk about.

I lost track of how many times I had to watch people's uncomfortable reactions when I answered, "Well, I was laid off, so now I'm in between jobs." I learned how to become more confident in answering gracefully, but it was emotionally draining. One time, I walked away from a group conversation because I knew I was next to share about my job and I did not have the mental or emotional energy to explain yet again.

As I have grown, I have learned to feel less shame in answering truthfully, especially as it becomes more common to experience job transitions at some point in our lives. But at twenty-three years old, I was mortified and embarrassed to seem like such a failure already.

The waves of grief would crash into me at unpredictable times. One morning, I was making an omelet, and after sitting down at the kitchen table, I realized that everyone else was at work and there I was. Alone. Unemployed. Another day, I went on a run and knew that was the only activity I had planned that day. Once I reached the door to my apartment, I fell to my knees and cried. Other times, the mail brought evidence of the loss, such as receiving notifications about my student-loan payments or filing for unemployment benefits.

And there are other moments that no one can prepare you for or talks about, such as when you receive the package of personal belongings from your old desk. Crying on the floor of my apartment with this box of items next to me is a memory I honestly try to forget.

The three-month mark of being unemployed hit me hard. I had sent countless applications with no responses from any companies. I felt misunderstood by others and isolated because of my situation, especially because few peers could relate or even try to understand what losing a job was like. I was angry because it was not my choice to leave the company, yet my entire life had changed. I felt insecure and less valuable because I did not have a job.

Once I realized the impact on my sense of self, I knew I needed a mindset change. My identity went beyond that. A job—or lack of a job—did not define me.

As a society, we tend to overidentify with our profession or at least draw a lot of our value from it. With goals of success and achievement, we place a high worth on work and career. A career is not a bad thing to value, but it cannot define us. It is not our identity. Who we are is not limited to what we do. A job is a part of you, but it is not all of you.

## THE PLAGUE OF "SHOULD"

I also faced the reality of finances. I was thankful for the unemployment checks, but it was barely enough to survive on. Because I supported myself financially, I needed to start making an income again. Soon.

After three months, I finally heard back from a company. I interviewed for the position and received a job offer all in a matter of weeks. Even though I wanted to step back and ensure the job aligned with my skills and career goals, I felt immense pressure to secure employment.

The day I received the job offer, I wrote in my journal: *Right now, to be honest, I feel trapped and that I should take the offer. I feel a little uneasy. A little trapped because what does it mean to say no to an offer . . .*

When I told my family, they were very excited but commented on the lack of enthusiasm in my voice. I felt like I had no option. I should focus on the need to pay my bills rather than my desire for a more exciting job. I should not turn down a salaried position. These internalized "shoulds" crowded the other voice that was quietly saying, "Is this what you really want to do?"

I didn't think I could ask myself that question. I felt guilty even contemplating my response to this offer when I knew how hard it was to receive one in the first place. How could I turn down a full-time job when I needed one?

I hesitantly accepted the job. I was relieved to know I would make an income again. I tried to be optimistic, especially since the position was described as a writing and creative role.

Within days after starting the role, however, it became obvious the reality of the job was not at all how it had been described in the interview. What I was told would be a creative and content role consisted of at least 70 percent data entry. My instincts had been right.

I knew the role was not a good fit, but admitting that made me feel guilty, because at least I had a job again. I knew what it was like to have no income, so I felt I should be content that I at least had a salary. I did not, and perhaps could not, let real emotions be felt yet. I numbed myself to anything other than gratitude for my employment and relief to again have a routine and paycheck. After the trauma of a sudden job loss, I had made this decision for my financial security.

Thankfully, I was involved with a variety of activities outside of work. I was training for the Chicago marathon, watching the Chicago Cubs win the World Series, and traveling for the holiday season. The months passed quickly, and I was happy in my life outside of work, so I didn't dwell on the fact I was unhappy at work.

That is, until I was home for Christmas when my brother asked me, "So how's the new job?"

I replied, "I'm content."

"So you hate it?"

I had a job. I was grateful. How could I be unhappy after I'd survived months of unemployment? How could I wish to change jobs when I'd just started this one? Embarrassed by my sense of shame and my fear of judgment, I did not let myself admit what I was actually feeling: miserable.

That would change in the new year. As I wrote out my goals and hopes, I realized I was far from where I wanted to be in my career. I had, I felt, taken a step backward in the wrong direction. I had taken a job for a paycheck, which I'd never thought I would do—especially because this job did not pay much.

I began to allow myself to feel and think about what I had been suppressing for the last five months. The impact of losing my first job resurfaced. The thoughts started swirling . . .

*Why did I accept this job? This is worse.*
*I'm so behind. My career looks like a failure.*
*Why did all this have to happen?*
*I feel so lost and directionless.*

As I started permitting myself to feel those emotions, I began to see with more clarity the reality of my present situation. Not only were there negative aspects about the position, but the environment was also toxic. I finally acknowledged to myself and others that the job was not a good fit and I needed to make a change.

I visited my brother in Los Angeles one weekend, and we sat in his car chatting. When I told him I felt like a failure, he laughed—and then turned to look at me and saw my face was serious. "Cate," he said. "You can't be hard on yourself for having accepted a job because you needed a paycheck. You could've kept looking, and when you'd interview, they'd ask what you were doing for the past eight months. What would you say? 'Oh, I was just waiting for the right opportunity?' Now you can say, 'I accepted a job to support myself, but now I'm looking for something long term, which is why I'm so interested in this company.'"

He reminded me that even though I'd made a practical decision, it did not ruin my chances of ever getting a different job in the future. I was letting fear take over my thoughts, believing my career trajectory was ruined.

Losing a job early in a career can feel debilitating. Without years of work experience, connections, and references, it is not easy to get back on your feet. That isolation made me feel even more stuck. With a naturally optimistic personality, I try to look for the good in every situation. Positivity is one of my strengths. And yet I was losing my sense of optimism about my own professional growth.

My optimism only continued to fade as I watched a few teammates quit the company I worked for. It was time to focus on my own job search to find a different job. I filled out countless applications and wrote cover letter after cover letter. Five months passed before I found a job that aligned well with my skills and passions. I thought it was too good to be true. Based on the job description and my knowledge about the organization, it felt like a dream. My application resulted in an interview. After I interviewed, I wanted the job even more.

Friends who heard me talk about the opportunity said, "Cate, I've never seen you this excited about a job".

And then I received the dreaded email saying the position had been offered to someone else.

Disappointed, I was angry I'd let myself hope it could potentially work out. I felt discouraged that my career was not heading in the right direction—or really in any direction at all. I felt overwhelmed at the reality of having to continue to work in an unhealthy environment.

Job loss was an especially sensitive issue for me because I watched my dad struggle with unemployment for years after the financial crisis in 2008. He was still without a full-time job. I grew up witnessing the devastating impacts of unemployment and career loss, and now I was experiencing it firsthand. The deep-rooted sense of failure, the heavy burden of discouragement, and the fear of financial instability were too much to bear at times.

During those dark moments, my faith kept me going. I needed to hope in something greater than myself or my circumstances to keep moving forward. I wanted to believe that good could come from all the disappointment. I needed to believe that. I had to trust and hope that the circumstances must all be a part of a greater plan I could not yet see.

I met with a counselor. I wanted to process the initial traumatic layoff experience, but I also worked through how the layoff affected my self-esteem and how the disappointments of my second job discouraged me even more.

When I was first laid off, some friends offered clichés such as, "When one door closes, another opens" or "Good things are around the corner." Said with the best intentions, these comments often benefit the person who says it rather than the one who hears it. Intended to make me feel better, these phrases are often said to move past the discomfort of not knowing what to say or how to help. Also, these comments can be empty promises that often lead to a false hope. I expected something positive to happen soon after my layoff when, in reality, I ended up in an even more disappointing situation.

Life often leaves us feeling, and being, out of control. Feeling powerless left me hesitant and fearful of taking proactive action. Counseling helped me realize how deeply stuck I felt. I'd never wanted my life to look like this—with a layoff and a toxic second job. A major takeaway from counseling was realizing how much I lived according to my own image of success, or what I think society views as success. Another major insight was evaluating how I respond to challenges and realizing how a desire for control looks different for everyone. I realized that many of the trials and difficult circumstances I faced growing up were not tied to my own decisions but decisions of others that affected me. I learned to cope by becoming adaptable.

While there is strength in adapting to events and changes, my weakness is in being passive within my own life. As a type-B personality who is more go-with-the-flow, there are times where I should take more initiative. I felt like I had no options available, but my counselor helped me see that I did, in fact, have more options. With that realization, I began to feel empowered to start taking more ownership over the direction of my life.

After a month of counseling, praying, and thinking through the potential consequences, I decided to quit my job. I never thought I would quit a job without a new one lined up, especially after knowing what it felt like to lose one, but I needed to leave that toxic work environment. I wanted to focus on writing this manuscript, so I decided to find a short-term job as a nanny or barista to pay my bills and support myself in the meantime. I wanted to take time off to step back and evaluate my career trajectory instead of feeling stuck in a job I had desperately accepted after being laid off. I did not want to simply jump into a new opportunity. Instead, I would be thoughtful about what I chose next.

My last day in the office was the day before my twenty-fifth birthday—a true quarter-life crisis. While I knew there was more uncertainty ahead, it was the first time in a long time that I felt excited to start a new chapter and hopeful for my future.

## CHAPTER 2

# COFFEE BEANS AND SHATTERED DREAMS

"The answer lies in our willing acceptance
of unwanted and unfortunate circumstances
even as we still cling to a radiant hope."

DR. MARTIN LUTHER KING JR.

With this new flexible schedule, I worked from my parents' house on the initial draft of this manuscript. I wrote for twelve to fifteen hours a day, sometimes staying up until 3:00 or 4:00 a.m. working on it.

Weeks later, I returned to Chicago and started a job as a barista at a high-end coffee company downtown. I loved coffee shops and thought it would be a good opportunity to work at one. My plan was to work there full-time to supplement my income as I continued working on the manuscript.

I had no idea what I was stepping into as a barista, especially at one of the most prestigious coffee bars in Chicago. I was amazed at how much attention to detail and precise tasks were involved in providing a cup of coffee. My location was in the heart of downtown near tourist locations, so it was constantly busy with a never-ending line—especially on the weekends—and no break in customers for hours.

My first day consisted of training and tasting various types of coffee. I quickly realized how little I knew about the art of a good brew. Over the next few shifts, I shadowed coworkers to learn their roles at the cash register, dishes, and bar-backing stations. The company took its training seriously. Typically, it takes a year to be approved to work at the milk-steaming station. No latte art for me.

Before I was cleared to brew any pour-over coffee, I spent weeks collecting inventory, washing dishes, and mopping floors. It was a humbling experience as I was constantly told how to fit into their workflow. This place was a well-oiled machine, and I needed to learn how to be a part of it. From learning how to save ten seconds by picking up glasses a certain way to using the sanitation machine, I tried my best to have a learner's mindset.

The first weeks were physically, mentally, and emotionally draining. It was most challenging not interacting with any customers, or rarely any people at all. My initial eight-hour shifts were spent in the back washing dishes until my hands were raw. The only exposure to people occurred when I took the next load of dishes from the bar area back to the kitchen to be cleaned. I looked forward to when the sanitizer finished its cycle so I could walk out and have an ounce of human contact.

Being alone with my thoughts and not engaging with people was a dangerous time for an extrovert like me—especially for one who was already wrestling with a lot of discouragement and self-doubt. There I was: a twenty-five-year-old college graduate. I'd begun my post-grad life working at a global PR agency, and now I was mopping floors and washing dishes.

Even though I had chosen to quit the corporate job, I did not realize how challenging it was to be a barista, especially at this location. Not to mention the hours of the shifts. At first, my schedule had no regular rhythms, so I might have an opening shift (6:00 a.m. to 2:00 p.m.) followed by a closing shift (2:00 p.m. to 9:00 p.m.) the next day. Later, my schedule started to level out and I regularly worked the opening shifts. At first, I thought that schedule would be ideal to have the afternoon to work on my book, but it proved to wear on me physically. As a night owl, I tried my best to go to bed before midnight, but I still needed to wake up at 4:30 a.m. to catch a bus downtown. I helped open the store, so I did not have time to eat breakfast. And although working the early shift gave me a thirty-minute break at 10:00 a.m., there was not quite enough time for lunch either. Due to the busy nature of the shifts, I often forgot to drink water.

Between getting four to six hours of sleep, standing on my feet all day, rarely eating real meals, and becoming increasingly dehydrated, I experienced my lowest sense of physical capacity. By the end of my shift, I was exhausted.

Working a different schedule than the rest of my friends was difficult emotionally. The timing of the shifts made me miss out on birthday dinners, church events, and parties. I missed seeing my friends regularly, which only contributed to increased feelings of isolation.

After weeks of dishwashing and collecting inventory, I was finally approved to work at the cash register where I was able to build relationships with customers. I highly value collaboration and working with people, so once I could engage with others, my time there dramatically improved. With positive feedback from coworkers and managers came more confidence. Soon, I knew the names and orders of the regular customers.

My experience continued to improve once I was trained to brew pour-over coffee. My shifts changed from eight hours of dishes and inventory to four hours of working at the register and four hours brewing pour overs. No longer was I always in the back, removed from the main purpose of the coffee shop.

Despite enjoying the shifts more, I knew it was not a sustainable position for me. I wanted time to focus on my book, but I had no energy left to focus on it. While the pay would get me by, eleven dollars an hour was not sustainable long term, especially living in a large city. I continued to work at the coffee shop, but pivoted again to look for a full-time, salaried job.

I submitted applications and was met with occasional interviews. Still, doors closed yet again. I hesitated to tell anyone about a potential job because I was tired of sharing the disappointing news. And then suddenly, an opportunity began to unfold.

A small marketing agency that works with nonprofit and social-impact clients needed a graphic designer. The position combined my creative skills and communications experience with my desire to have purpose-driven work. It seemed too good to be true. After several rounds of interviews and a design test, I was offered the job.

After a year and a half, it felt surreal to foster a sense of hope about my career again. There was so much joy as I shared the news with friends and family, especially my friends who had walked closely with me since the layoff. They surprised me one night to celebrate. My job situation was finally changing for the better.

The CEO and I selected a start date and finalized details about my arrival. I was invited to the holiday party. They purchased my computer. They even asked me what kind of pens I wanted to have at my desk.

Days later, I was at a coffee shop with a friend, telling her all about how grateful I was for the new opportunity. I checked my phone and saw that I had a missed call and voice mail from the co-owner of the company. I also saw a notification for an email with the subject line *Offer*.

My heart dropped.

I opened the email to read the words, "I am writing in regard to the conditional offer we sent you. We need to look in a different direction and determined we have to rescind your offer of employment."

*How could this be happening?*

*Had I just lost another job?*

My friend who had stepped away for a moment came back to find me in tears. All I could do was show her my phone. We walked out of the coffee shop; I cried on the sidewalk. She accompanied me home. I walked in a haze, shocked and heartbroken. I did not care how I looked at that moment as I fumbled along a major street in Chicago, sobbing.

At my apartment, I sent a few texts to family and friends and started to slowly process the loss that was now my reality. Again.

A few days later, I returned to my parents' home in Virginia for the holidays. In a time typically surrounded by gifts, blessings, and Christmas miracles, I dealt with grief and yet another job loss. I hated feeling the way I did, but I was hurting. I was mourning.

My parents assured me I could work through the loss however I needed to process it. We had quality time as a family for the next few days, but that did not keep me from crying at the dinner table one night as I tried to explain how lost and discouraged I felt. Once I had finally felt hope for my career again, it was shattered.

I returned to Chicago right before New Year's Eve at probably the lowest I had felt in my life. I'd had all these ideas of what my year was going to look like with the new job. I had left my job at the coffee shop before the offer was rescinded, so I returned to the city with no guaranteed income.

I began that year with overwhelming plans for . . . nothing. At that point, would I even stay in Chicago? My life had, yet again, been ripped from under me.

Facing unemployment again was unbearable to me, so I took the job search to a whole other level. I put writing this book on hold and focused solely on submitting applications and writing cover letters. I created an Excel spreadsheet that tracked every job I applied for, which ended up at over three hundred jobs. Within the spreadsheet, I listed the category of the job, the application status, and if I knew any contacts. I wanted to work strategically as best I could to find a new position.

I lost track of the phone interviews, in-person interviews, and rejection emails. Honestly, I became numb to it all. I remember describing my strengths during phone interviews as if I was reading a script. With all the practice, I knew what to say, but deep down I struggled to believe it.

I completed a few freelance design projects. While it was not a salary by any means, I was grateful to survive and hope for a long-term job. I did not want to make the same mistake of jumping into something without careful consideration and understanding of what I thought about the role and company.

This job searching lasted over three months. I sent hundreds of applications and countless emails. I reached out to contacts, former colleagues, and friends. I was doing my best, open to whatever could happen.

## COMMUNITY VS. CAREER

Due to the sheer volume of applications I submitted, there were quite a few opportunities that began to move forward. Interestingly, all of the potential jobs were in other cities, but nothing was progressing in Chicago. At the time, I had been living in Chicago for almost three years. I did not want to move away. There were a lot of contributing factors to that, such as wanting my career to be restored in Chicago and not wanting to lose the community I had worked so hard to build.

I also began to understand the value of being rooted somewhere. By the time I finished high school, I had attended six different schools. I went to college in a different state. I spent a summer interning in Nashville. I graduated college and moved to Chicago knowing only two people.

I was fully capable of making new friends in a new city but felt a desire to keep investing in one place. I felt discouraged when I thought about leaving this city I'd come to call home. I was not against moving, but I wanted to do so on my own terms and for a job I was excited about. I also feared leaving Chicago meant my career had failed there.

Yet at that point in my career, I was more desperate for work than ever before. I did not want to be completely close minded to the idea of moving, even if it meant choosing my career over community. So I kept my options open and was met with offers in various cities and even another country.

One position at a nonprofit would have led me back to North Carolina, but it did not offer health insurance. Another job would have involved a move to a rural area in East Africa, which I would have done in a heartbeat after college. At this point, however, I did not think I was in the best place emotionally and mentally to uproot my entire life and culture.

More than during my previous times of unemployment, I had several interviews and opportunities moving forward all at the same time. Was my spreadsheet paying off? One possibility caught my attention: a design position at a prestigious consulting firm. In fact, the recruiter reached out to me because of an application I had sent months before the rescinded offer.

After over four rounds of interviews, I received the offer. I could not believe it. This company wanted me, despite my rollercoaster of a résumé.

Sounds like a no brainer, right? The firm was building out an in-house team, so this role would require a relocation to Atlanta. To work collaboratively with the team on the West Coast, the hours would be 11:00 a.m. to 7:00 p.m. Initially, that sounded ideal for my night-owl self, but as I thought more about it, I knew the schedule would make it challenging to make new friends in a different city. Still, with the quality of the offer from the company, I was conflicted. Should I pick up and leave the community I had spent the last three years building? Should I move to a new city and choose prioritizing my career over having availability for friendships, volunteering, and my community?

Although I was given twenty-four hours to decide, I asked for more time so I could visit the city. Thankfully, they accommodated me. I went to Atlanta where the company welcomed me with open arms. I had lunch with members of the team I would join. I toured the office. I even looked at potential apartments to get a feel for what my life could look like there.

I went into that weekend with an open mind, having no idea what I would choose on the other end. I sought counsel, prayed, and thought a lot about the decision and its potential impacts on my life. I journaled a lot so I could be very aware and honest with my thoughts and motivations, fears, and desires.

I realized I was letting the past disappointments in Chicago keep me from hoping my career could improve in the future. I was losing faith that things could change and thinking that moving to Atlanta would be my one and only shot at a career again.

Before I went into the weekend, I mostly thought I would end up moving to Atlanta. While I was there, however, I began entertaining the idea of, "What if I said no?" It made me question whether I wanted to secure job stability with the offer right in front of me or whether to hope for something to open up in Chicago.

During the visit, there were little moments that helped me process this decision. For instance, when I talked to Uber or Lyft drivers, I happened to be in the cars of individuals who were tired of the city and did not have positive things to say about Atlanta. One even asked where I was from, and when I said Chicago, his face lit up. He talked about how much he loved that city.

Then, after lunch with my potential coworkers, we walked back to the office, and I asked one of the guys what he thought of Atlanta. He said he absolutely loved his job and working for the company, but he had moved from somewhere else and did not like living in Atlanta. Now, don't get me wrong; Atlanta is a fantastic city. But I wondered, was now the right time for me to start over again?

As I thought about how I would invest in a new community, I knew working until at least seven every evening would hinder me from focusing on relationships. If I moved, the relocation would be for my career, not leaving much flexibility for other commitments. But at the same time, could I turn down a great job opportunity?

Compared to when I accepted the first job offer after being laid off, this time, I acknowledged how I desire people's approval and acceptance. I admitted to myself that I was fearful of being judged for turning down this job offer, but I did not want those fears to hold too much weight in the decision. Instead of feeling pressured by what I felt like I should do or what I thought others expected of me, I ultimately chose what was best for me at that time.

Between my desire to stay in Chicago and the value I placed on the community, I wanted to stay and fight for my career to be restored in Chicago. So, I decided to turn down a great job opportunity. I said no to Atlanta to say yes to Chicago, even if it meant perpetuating the uncertainty.

## HOLDING ON TO HOPE

While I was in Atlanta considering the job offer, I made time for a phone interview with a company in Chicago—#151 on my spreadsheet, to be exact. The role sounded interesting, but it was early in the process. I focused my attention on the decision I had in front of me. A week after I turned down the Atlanta offer, I was invited for an in-person interview with this company.

In preparing for the interview, I realized it was a unique opportunity in which the requisite skills and experiences aligned with my own. I was awed by the office design, impressed by the talent of the agency, and encouraged by the warmth of the people I met. During my interview, I discussed how the role fit my strengths and used my experiences from previous jobs in a way I had not seen before. I walked out of the office after the interview beaming, thinking to myself, *I want to work there!*

A week later, I was asked to complete a writing and design exercise. Two weeks passed without hearing anything. Then I finally heard that the team wanted one final in-person interview.

I met with multiple people from different departments and thoroughly enjoyed the two hours of meetings. They were still interviewing final candidates, but due to vacation schedules, I would not hear back for almost three weeks. By this point, I really wanted the job. I knew that if I ended up with the job offer, the wait and delay of income would be worth it in the end.

Those weeks felt extraordinarily long. I battled against a lot of fear and uncertainty. I prayed for the job to work out. I was afraid of another no, but I let myself hope for a yes.

Three weeks later, I learned I was their first-choice candidate. Without question, I accepted the offer and started work immediately.

As I reflect, this was the job that restored my career, not just in Chicago but in general. For two years I had believed my plans were off in the abyss. I had to rebuild a lot of what was lost financially, emotionally, and professionally; however, my career was finally in a position of redemption.

\* \* \*

Now that you know my story, you also know why I became passionate about writing this book. Before the age of twenty-six, I had experienced a layoff, a toxic work environment, a minimum-wage job, a rescinded offer, and multiple rounds of unemployment. I could never have imagined my career would unfold the way it did after graduating college. But even though I often felt isolated in my own circumstances, I knew I was not the only one struggling. And I did not want anyone else to suffer in silence.

The unique adjustment from college into adulthood is a pivotal transition in our lives. Thrown into the realities of life, we are forced to learn some basic truths, often starkly different from what we expected. Yet what we learn during these years prepares us for the uncertainty, challenges, and decisions we will face throughout the rest of our lives.

## CHAPTER 3

# FRESHMAN YEAR OF LIFE

"Appreciate this moment. Stop and look around you. Be thankful for all you have and where you are because this time next year, nothing will be the same."

R.H. SIN

For the first two decades of our lives, we spent most of our time in the highly structured environment of the school system.

We knew the routine of the school day.

We knew the drills of classes, homework, and tests.

We knew one school year would be followed by another.

We transitioned from one level of school to the next without too much disruption. We understood the system: kindergarten to elementary school, then middle or junior high school to high school. The path was laid out before us, and we followed it. And most of us did not even question why.

It was not until our senior year of high school that we were first faced with what to do afterward. College was often an expected next step—two thirds of high school students enroll in college immediately following high-school graduation.[2] However, one third of high-school students may pursue a gap year, the military, or other alternative paths. The linear extension of formal education after high school is not the only option for graduating students.

A gap year can provide a built-in time for students to participate in an internship or apprenticeship, work or travel abroad, or volunteer. Internships, while often unpaid, are valuable hands-on learning opportunities and provide insight for a career direction. Apprenticeships are paid career-training programs where students learn on the job and in classroom settings to work in specific industries such as construction and other trades, manufacturing, health care, finance, telecommunications, and transportation.[3]

Another alternative is community college, which provides opportunities for transferring or career training. With rising tuition costs and student loan debt, some students may choose to complete an associate's degree at a local school before transferring to earn a bachelor's degree at another college or university. Community college can also provide career and skills-based training for students who want to enter the workforce immediately after high school graduation.

Similarly, technical college or trade schools specialize in career-driven courses teaching skills that apply to specific careers.[4] If you already know what career you want to pursue, such as carpentry, electrical work, or coding, your education helps to springboard you into that field.

For many high school graduates, the military presents an appealing option for not only a career but also as an alternative route to gain skills through on-the-job training. Advantages to joining the military include a salary, room and board, paid college tuition through the GI Bill, and retirement benefits after twenty years.[5] With its diverse branches and areas of service, the military is a respected route after high school or college.

A traditional four-year college experience may not be the best decision for everyone; however, it is the pathway for the majority of students. This book focuses on life after college, but the stories, truths, and messages will apply to you whether you extended your education at a college or university or whether you jumped straight into the working world. Regardless of how you stepped out of the academic setting, stepping into the working world for the first time is a pivotal transition.

To understand the tumultuous nature of our twenties and how we are impacted, we need to consider *why* it is such a pivotal and unique time in our lives. Even if you've been out of the school system for several years, I urge you to read this chapter reflecting on how you felt when you began your journey into post-grad life. I guarantee you will glean wisdom from those who shared their stories that can help you in current circumstances.

Most seniors at universities live in the tension of two worlds: their present college experience and the looming specter of post-grad life. Seniors can live in graduation denial, as if their college experience will never end, and at the same time be caught up in the excitement and anticipation of what is next. Naturally, this dichotomy of emotions impacts their friendships, academic life, and career search.

Whether they acknowledge this or not, most seniors are aware of these two worlds and how this tension affects their last year of college. As one survey participant, Tierney, shared, "On the one hand, I'm really excited to see what's next in store. On the other hand, I'm not quite ready to let go of [college] and the great people and memories here." Becca, another survey respondent, agreed. "Not knowing what I was doing after grad was hard, and feeling the added pressure that all of our friends were about to scatter created a lot of tension."

Students often struggle to balance living in the present and enjoying time with friends while also focusing their attention on developing their future plans. Senior year can feel uniquely strange and isolating compared to the rest of college because you are focused on cherishing social activities, completing your academic career, and applying for jobs, all while determining your next steps after graduation. Academics during this final year can be particularly challenging because the course load involves higher-level classes including senior seminars, capstone projects, or research. Those courses are valuable, but it can be tempting to check out as a student. With major life decisions ahead of you, the focus on day-to-day schoolwork becomes that much more difficult. How do you focus on writing a paper when you are trying to secure a salary?

Many graduating seniors understand this conflict, especially when they have a sense of direction for their post-grad plans. "The hardest part is finding the motivation to keep going," said Justin. "I am so close to going to law school and fully working on the startup—two things that I am incredibly passionate and interested in—that it's hard to get myself to sit down and study/do homework for classes that seem silly to me right now."

As a student, it is your job to manage the deadlines of papers or projects and exams set by the semester's syllabi. As you prepare for a career, however, your efforts shift to applications, networking, and practicing for interviews.

Perspective continues to shift as the realities of job searching become apparent. To enhance résumés and gain further industry experience, many seniors complete semester internships on top of their classes. Other students work part time to save money before graduating. For some majors, the balancing act is often paired with working full time in clinicals or in schools. As Chelsea shared, "It was hard to balance student teaching my second semester with the rest of senior life. Many of my friends and roommates were part-time students, going out on weeknights and sleeping in most days, whereas I pretty much had a full-time 7:00 a.m. to 3:00 p.m. job every day. Although I loved it, it took extra effort to find time for friends and to not envy others and their free time."

The change between the fall semester and spring is almost palpable. The fall semester is typically marked with a heavier workload and a focus on spending time with friends and investing in organizations. When the spring semester starts, though, time becomes more limited, and you likely feel overwhelmed with the uncertainty of what you will do after graduation. You are bombarded with everyone's favorite question: "What are you doing after graduation?" As Dessie reflected, "It also was stressful to deal with the pressure I felt to have an impressive enough job lined up. Everyone asks what you're doing when you graduate, and it felt like there were a lot of judgments tied to your answer."

Well-intentioned professors and other students often ask about post-graduation plans. While their questions often stem from curiosity, it becomes increasingly difficult to answer when you have no response to give. In the waiting game, you may be left for months anticipating results about a job, fellowship, or graduate program. "I was torn to shreds waiting to hear back from law schools and waiting to get my LSAT scores," said Imani. "All I could think about was what if I didn't get in anywhere, what if I wasn't smart enough, etc. I knew it would all work out, but the stress of it all and the uncertainty was so hard."

In these times of waiting, it may help to prepare a short response so you can be ready to give an answer when the post-graduation-plan question comes. Because it will. Several times. You might say, "Not yet, but I'm excited to see what happens." Or "I'm networking and looking into opportunities." It is normal to feel overwhelmed and insecure when asked about your plans after graduation. If you have a response prepared, you'll feel more empowered and less anxious when the question arises.

The reality of graduation sinks in even deeper once the post-graduation announcements start. Friends accept jobs. Your roommate decides on a grad school. Your classmate selects a fellowship program. Slowly but surely, plans begin to unfold.

## THE FLOOD OF STATUS UPDATES

As May approaches, you may feel you are the last student standing, uncertain of what you'll be doing or where you'll be living (or both). Your area of study or desired industry will influence when the job search begins. I remember hearing updates from friends and classmates during the fall semester and being shocked (and a bit jealous) that they already knew what they were doing. Their jobs were secured, their cities decided, their salaries known.

Most fields of work, however, do not hire nine months in advance. A graduate who now works in recruiting said, "I wish I knew that not having a job upon graduating was normal, and outside of the business world, no one gets offered [a job] months in advance. I'm the one hiring recent grads now, and I need people to start immediately." Maya explained, "We hardly look at résumés until people graduate. Applying to jobs while still in school, at least in my field, is pointless . . . but of course all you look at is the business majors who got offered jobs in August before senior year and wonder what you're doing wrong."

As you compare yourself to your friends and peers, it is easy to wonder whether you are trying hard enough or are good enough. Social media does not help. Especially during spring semester, you are confronted several times a day with yet another friend who has posted a status about accepting a job offer.

During my senior year, I wrote on my blog, "Like many of my fellow senior (and especially jobless) friends, I have begun to feel that I am behind. Delayed. Waiting. While everyone else is moving forward." As I watched more friends gain certainty in their future, I could not help but feel the weight of my own uncertainty.

Even though not all my peers knew what they were doing after graduation, the social media posts can make it seem as though *everyone* knows but you. Blake explained, "A lot of my friends were pursuing jobs in the finance/banking sector and were getting job offers before the school year had even started." In a different industry, he tried not to compare herself to them, but it proved to be difficult. "I felt a little behind . . . and a lot of pressure to find a 'prestigious' job."

"They know where they're going to be living, they can start looking for housing and roommates, they know that they'll have steady income, and they can relax for the rest of the year," said Marie. "It's hard to feel so uncertain about your future when people around you are already all set."

Even if it feels like everyone is accepting jobs, there are plenty of individuals who are also waiting. As Amanda said, "It was discouraging to watch others accept jobs or get accepted to grad school when I was simply waiting in the wings. I had a promising position that ended up not working out at the last minute, which was extremely discouraging. This led me to be hard on myself and question if I was truly cut out for this competitive industry."

"When I didn't know what I was doing post-grad and all these people around me were getting jobs, I honestly just felt stuck." Mark said. "Every time I heard that someone else had figured out their next step, my stomach would flip."

It is natural to let disappointments cloud our view of ourselves. Do not allow watching others announce plans make you feel worse about yourself or second guess what you have to offer. Your time will come.

You may graduate with no idea of what to do after the summer. You may graduate deciding to move to a city without a job. You may graduate with your plans fully developed or not developed at all. Whatever the case, those decisions unfold into your own unique story.

## BUILD YOUR OWN STORY

More than ever before, we live in a highly globalized world. Technology provides flexibility and creative ways to work—the world is truly at our fingertips. In this digital age, we have more choices and potential directions for how our lives could unfold.

For the generations before us, after graduating high school or college, they would typically stay in the area or return to where they grew up to find work or to get married. Now, because of the digital age, it is common for students to move to an entirely new city or state, or even to a different country. The expanded choices can be both exciting and intimidating.

"For the longest time, deciding where I truly belong made it so hard for me to decide where to apply and what to do next. I felt absolutely lost/confused/excited all the time!" Mona shared. "I mean how do you ever settle when suddenly everything in the world is an option?"

In my personal circle alone, I had friends move to various states and regions of the United States, in addition to friends moving to South America, Europe, Asia, and Africa. With the knowledge that we can do anything anywhere, ironically, students can often feel paralyzed by the many potential options.

"There's no specific field I'm supposed to work in with an English major, so the wide openness was scary," Tasha said. Rather than let that paralyze her, she followed her sense of adventure and moved to another country to teach English for a few years.

Even if you had a major that provided direction for job options, you may still wonder about other options or second-guess your decision. The trick is to embrace your expanded choices. "My current career path is to work on drug development in a chemistry lab," Kylie said, "but I'd also be just as happy opening a cupcake bakery or living off the grid in the rainforest."

Sometimes, it may be a matter of not what, but when. After Jasmine was rejected from grad programs, she struggled to know what she should do instead. "I had no idea what I was doing next in my life, and that really bothered me. Being rejected from grad school was a stab in my gut. No one likes rejection, but especially from your top school—it physically hurts." While that was a painful and trying year, she applied for graduate programs again and was accepted into her top choice the following year.

You may intentionally choose a path that looks different from your peers. "To be honest, I had no intention of going straight to my career path right after graduation," Sam said. "I saved up some money in the summer to travel and work for one year. I have plenty of time to start my career path. No need to start after graduation when there is so much of the world to see."

It takes courage to listen to your own values and goals amidst the societal and internal expectations, especially if you choose a path that is not standard. There is no cookie-cutter way or time in which to secure a job. And despite the various options and approaches to life after college, there *will* come a point in the year when you decide about your post-grad plans. Whether it is accepting a job, internship, or fellowship, or accepting that you will move home to look for jobs—at some point, you will make that decision.

"I was happy I graduated without a job because that left my doors open for opportunity and gave me time to figure out what I wanted to do," said Adrienne. She did not feel pressured to find a job, and instead she moved to South America and worked abroad. Within a year, she started her own company.

There is no way you can fully know how a decision will impact your life. That is part of the risk. It is beneficial to think critically about decisions, but there is no way to know how it will unfold. Like it or not, you do not see the whole picture, and you cannot know how one experience could lead to the next. I moved to Chicago with no concept of how long I would live in the city. I acknowledged the unknowns but was excited about the next step.

As graduation draws near, a strong sense of excitement and anticipation for what lies ahead also emerges. "I think that the future is incredibly exciting, and I never understood why people say college is the best years of your life," Jayden said. "I have had an amazing time at [my college] and wouldn't change it for the world, but I genuinely think this is just the beginning, and I cannot wait to see what the world has in store for me."

It is exhilarating to think about all the new experiences and possibilities in store for your life after graduation. Just the idea of a limitless future is exciting. After all, you spent years of your life preparing for it. Graduating seniors often mentioned their excitement for independence, to be on their own, and to move into a new city. For many, this marks the first time they will live somewhere on their own.

"I am really looking forward to living in a city," Marie said. "I love that DC has an abundance of sights to see, museums to explore, restaurants to eat at, and exciting nightlife."

"My college served as a preparation and a bridge into embracing New York. I was excited for a bigger pond, to see how far I could stretch myself in a new place, to see where this fellowship and LGBTQIA-adoring environment would lead me," Dan said. "I was excited to find myself all over again."

For those who choose to move abroad, graduates look forward to the sense of adventure ahead. "I was really excited about living in a new country that I had never been to," Olive said. "Trying new foods, seeing new sights, figuring out how to live in a totally foreign place."

Beyond the thrill of exploring a new place, students begin to anticipate what it would be like to launch their careers. After taking years of classes in a particular practice area, they are energized to test the theories and perspectives in the real world. "I was most excited about making it on my own," said Michelle. "I had been preparing for twenty-two years of my life to become a teacher and to live on my own. I was excited to have my name on a classroom door and for a class to actually be *mine!*"

"Graduating college, in and of itself, was an exhilarating, relieving and really meaningful experience for me," recalled Ruth. "I was ready to break the student mold and actually live out the different concepts and viewpoints I was absorbing in the classroom and apply my skills to a profession/population I cared deeply about."

Graduation can also be a time to reflect on the changes that have occurred within you. For the first time in your life, you are fully owning the decisions for yourself and your future. That sense of ownership can lead to greater self-confidence. "I felt accomplished, educated, and confident," TJ said. "I was happy to have a job with a good salary, and to move to a new city with unlimited possibilities. This was my time to make what I wanted out of my life."

There is a sense of relief when you decide what your plans are for after graduation. That next step, however, is not deciding the rest of your life. It feels all-consuming in college because so much of the future is unknown, but there will be additional forks in the road ahead. Deciding what to do after college strengthens our decision-making skills and helps us mature as we practice for future decisions.

Mona, an international student, reflected on her experience. "Graduating is not just about getting the job or not. It's definitely more about a new journey of self-discovery, taking more risks, and making bold decisions when there is so much uncertainty in the air."

As you prepare to graduate, you make decisions for yourself about where you want to live, what you want to do, and who you want to be around. It can feel overwhelming, but also empowering to make decisions that shape your future. That sense of confidence only grows in your twenties as you take more ownership over your future, your career, and your relationships.

## GRADUATING TO BECOME A STUDENT OF LIFE

Ever since we began kindergarten, we functioned as students in structured environments. Each fall, we would start a new school year in a different grade with a new classroom and teacher. By the time May or June rolled around, the year was over and summer vacation began. We may not have realized it then, but we were accustomed to this rhythm of nine months of school and three long months of summer, where you could go to summer camp, work, travel, volunteer, or complete internships.

All of a sudden, with graduation, that structure disappears. Summer vacation? Gone. Designated fall and spring breaks? Unless you are a teacher, they are gone. Welcome to the nine-to-five life. You leave behind an academic calendar to join a cycle of working five days a week, every week, year round. You leave the safety and security of a college campus to live on your own in a new city or area. You go from meal plans and student discounts to becoming 100 percent financially responsible for yourself.

The first year out of college is one of the most uncomfortable, undirected, and overwhelming transitions that we experience. While the upcoming decade will contain many aspects of change, the first year of the journey is often the most difficult.

"What I didn't prepare for was how quickly things would change, or how I would have to grow more in the month after graduating versus the entirety of my college career," Whitney said. "I didn't think that being uncomfortable would feel more normal than being satisfied."

The loss of structure can feel unsettling. There may be a short gap between graduation and the start of a new job. Or there may be a longer time of uncertainty with no plans. Summer may feel familiar, like a previous summer internship, but when that first fall semester rolls around, it hits you differently.

"I knew I had an internship in DC for two months, so I had some semblance of what I would be doing for the summer . . . After the internship, I had what could be described as a quarter-life crisis . . . I returned home jobless." Josh continued, "All of my friends had moved away. I no longer had an end goal (graduation) to work toward. Even my family was vacationing. I really panicked and was terrified that my life wasn't going anywhere."

This story is not uncommon. There are many graduates who had a short-term plan but then did not know what would happen after that. Even though you knew the changes would occur and you talked about the idea of post-grad for months, the reality does not fully resonate until it is September and you're not going back.

"We know that college is a preparatory/self-exploratory rite of passage, and that it's much more than just high-school classes on steroids," said Gabriel. "But what's so difficult to grasp—which I witnessed firsthand, as most of us did—is that it's severely limited in its scope. Talking about post-grad life is a lot different than actually living it."

"The transition is much harder and much longer than I expected," Lori explained. "I don't think there's a ton you can do to prepare for it. Moving locations, making new friends, and learning a new job function will be hard no matter where you go."

Graduating college is the last major milestone that you complete in the company of a large group of people. While we grew up expecting to reach these milestones together, this is the first time we are introduced to how things are in the real world: friends enter various life stages and develop careers at different paces. It is clear *why* the initial transition into adulthood is so difficult: your entire world changes, and the structures in which you grew up are obliterated. You no longer follow the same path as your peers, and you are left to navigate everything mostly by yourself.

"College is life with a safety net," Meredith said. "After graduation the net would be taken away with financial, social, spiritual, professional, physical consequences. The trial run of making mistakes and trying new things without serious consequences if things didn't go well would soon be over. Scared me. Still does."

You leave college as a senior—only to become a freshman of life. You leave behind the achievements and status of a college senior to start all over again. Yet unlike in structured school environments, there are no orientation guides. There are no RAs. There are no upperclassmen volunteers. The first tentative steps will feel overwhelming, even difficult and isolating. But remember, you are not alone in this experience.

Lessons learned in the early transitional years are lessons we continue to learn and relearn throughout our twenties and beyond. While we no longer have an educational system guiding us, we can resolve to remain lifelong learners of the new independent world ahead of us.

## CHAPTER 4

# A NEW NORMAL

"The twenties are an inflection point–the great reorganization–a time when the experiences we have disproportionately influence the adult lives we will lead."

DR. MEG JAY

When my parents drove me to the airport two weeks after graduation, I did not know when I would return. I did not know if I would stay in Chicago beyond the summer. I did not know whether I would end up with a full-time job as a result. I did not know if I would even like living there. I boarded the plane with my two checked bags and my one-way ticket to a new life.

I had no idea what to expect from the move, and that is likely the case for many of you. If you move to a new city, state, or country, you will experience a wave of adjustments, and that is normal. Unfortunately, you will find that many recent graduates do not talk about it. People do not typically admit they are struggling. However, I found that once someone takes the risk to share, it gives freedom for others to open up too.

I left the life I knew at Elon University, where I walked around campus and constantly ran into people I knew, to the third largest city in the United States, realizing I knew no one. On the train, bus, streets, I initially expected to run into a familiar face like I did in college. But I soon realized that would not happen in Chicago, at least for some time.

While I drove to the grocery store in my car in college, I no longer had that luxury in Chicago. Living in a city without a car means you buy groceries at the closest store and walk or take public transportation back to your apartment.

My first outing consisted of a trip to Walmart Express to buy sheets, hangers, and a few other necessities. I walked a half mile to the bus stop from the apartment, rode the bus for 1.5 miles, and then walked into the store. As I bought my items, I realized whatever I bought I would have to carry myself.

I walked out of Walmart and into a storm. I hurried over to the bus stop to discover that the next bus would not arrive for at least fifteen minutes. I did not think to look at the weather before I left, so I had no jacket. There I was, standing in the rain and holding on to soaked shopping bags as I waited for the bus. Eventually, I hopped on the bus, and when I arrived back at my stop, it was raining even harder. As I stepped into puddles on my walk home, I laughed out loud, realizing that this was my new normal.

These are the types of moments we cannot anticipate or even articulate until they happen. If we move to a new city, many habits will be adjusted, routines will be altered, and comforts will be diminished. There is a learning curve, but it can also be empowering to handle all the changes that come with moving to a new city or town.

At the beginning of my time in Chicago, I wanted to familiarize myself with navigating around the city. I purposely wandered downtown and into other neighborhoods and used my love of coffee shops to explore the city. Without friends yet, I would go alone. Exploring

Chicago neighborhoods via coffee shops became my favorite way to see a new area of the city.

Let your loneliness push you to explore your new town or city. It is tempting to stay with what is familiar, but you do not need to spend hours watching Netflix in your bed. Challenge yourself to get out and explore your new city to make it feel like your home.

Many survey respondents reflected on the choice between the familiar and the unfamiliar, and what choosing the unknown would mean for their own personal growth. Sometimes these decisions happen for the first time right after graduation, and other times they could be years down the road.

Caroline grew up and went to college in Texas but debated what she wanted to do after graduation. "I went back and forth between staying in Texas and moving away," she said, "but I wanted to prove to myself that I could live outside of and away from everything I've ever known." Caroline ended up living in a large city for a few years after college and made a second move to another large city—both in different states.

Kathleen, on the other hand, knew she wanted to move to New York after graduation. "I had summer housing and a job at a retail store lined up, but that was it," she said. "It was pretty scary, but I felt prepared enough and confident that I'd land a job by the fall (I was wrong, I didn't land a job until January). For me, it was New York or bust, so I had to make it work!"

Another aspect of moving to a new place is realizing it could be temporary. Cities are known for being transient, which can be difficult when trying to invest in a new place. After all, making quality friendships looks different after college.

"People move, people move on and change. The rate you can get to know people is painfully slower than college," Trevor reflected. "You have to plan ahead anytime you want to hang out. It's not like you can call someone over on a whim to hang out when it's convenient for you.

It's also hard to build trust, explain more of your background that was likely a given for most kids you went to college with."

No matter when you move or how often you move, you will deal with similar circumstances and challenges. It is never easy to start over, and it will always take time to build a life and rhythms in a new place.

Gabrielle shared her struggle of living in a transient season while doing a nine-month apprenticeship. "I feel the desire and need to make my next step be a place where I can maybe plant some roots—a place where I can make friends and be confident that I will be there for a while. But then again, isn't this what being young and single is all about? Being able to move from place to place without anyone holding you back? It is this internal monologue I feel."

How much should you invest in your current environment when you are uncertain of how long you will be there? "So much changed during the first year of post-grad life." Madeline reflected. "I was still getting used to being married, we both graduated college, moved across the country twice in six months, lived in three apartments, and started new jobs."

Madeline said she was excited to explore a new city but felt stressed to be in a constant state of change while her husband was finishing his program. "Once we found out he passed, they gave him a list of cities across the country and a weekend to choose one. We went with Austin, Texas. Neither of us had ever been to Texas before. We packed up all our belongings again and drove our car and the moving truck all the way, finding hotels along the way, and not even signing a lease until a few days after we arrived. Since moving to Austin, I feel like this is exactly where we are meant to be."

You may move to a city with no intention of staying there and be surprised at your desire to stay, or you may jump from city to city. Place is important and it can be difficult when your location does not feel like home. "Not really feeling settled ended up being my biggest challenge," said Julie. "I didn't like the job or city I was in at first, and knowing that I wanted to move on from both of them sooner rather than later actually held me back from getting invested there and planting any roots . . . and a whole year without making friends outside of work or not liking your surroundings can really wear on you!"

A major part of this self-discovery is figuring out what kind of environment you want to live in, what kind of activities or amenities are important to you, and what kind of city or region is best for you. Living in different environments can reveal what you value about a pace of life, career opportunities, and communities. You can also learn what you would rather avoid, such as traffic, lack of parking, or no public transit system.

Honestly, I expected to live in Chicago for a short time and then move somewhere else to experience a new adventure. As I spent more time in that city, however, I saw my desires change. Even though I love having friendships all over the country, I began to see the value of investing deeply in one place over a period of time.

After living in Chicago for a few years, I watched my desires shift from wanting new experiences to enjoying the sense of home. I may not know how long I will be in Chicago, but my motto is, "Wherever you are, be all there." Even though I am not guaranteed to live here forever, I want to live intentionally, as if I knew it would be for a long time.

We were told to make the most of our college experience and that was only a few years, so why should we treat the rest of our life any differently?

## MAKE YOURSELF AT HOME

From when I crossed the graduation stage to when I passed through airport security, I had two weeks to prepare for my living situation.

In my typical type-B fashion, I did not know where I was living until three days before I flew to Chicago. Just in time, I found an opportunity to sublet an apartment from local college students for the summer.

My situation, while ideal at the time for a fresh graduate, was a stark change—from living with friends in college to living with strangers in a new city. By subletting, I knew both the place and the roommates were temporary. I had my own room, but I felt like a guest in someone else's home. I did not feel settled in Chicago until I rented an apartment of my own.

Any transition will include deciding how to make your new environment feel like home. Some may thrive living alone after college, but others may find it to be an abrupt change from living with roommates in college or being around family.

"This is the first time I am living alone," shared Val. "It's weird not to come home to another body, the smells from someone cooking dinner, the sounds of someone watching Netflix in their room. But at the same time, the sound of silence to me is the sound of growing up."

Hunter admitted he was not prepared for how hard moving to a new city would be. "So many friends moved back to their hometowns, and things were easy for them as they got to hang out with high school friends or had so many connections already in that area," he said. "I, for the most part, was starting from scratch, and that was difficult."

Many graduates I surveyed felt that living at home was a great way to save money and to have parental support during this major transition time. Camila lived at home and saved money while working before she moved abroad. "Having that support and security really made my life easier," she said. "I also never heard once from my parents that I should get a full-time job. They never pressured me. My mom was so excited for me to go with the flow and follow my heart and work in another country for a while."

For those taking board exams or other certifications, living at home provided the freedom to study, save money, and eventually look for a job. Ethan wanted to take a gap year before beginning pharmacy school. "I hadn't applied anywhere yet, and I hadn't found a job in the meantime, so I moved back home," he said. "It was pretty nerve-racking not to really know my next step. But being at home with the support of family definitely helped out."

On the other hand, others struggled to navigate living at home after living on their own for the past several years. As Anisa recalled, "I lived at home for four months, and it was really, really tough. I got in a bunch of arguments with my parents that I wouldn't have gotten in had I not been living with them again. Being away for four years and living at home again was really difficult."

Darrell agreed. "I loathed living at home just because I am a very independent person and my home life is very structured, which is great growing up, but not so much when you are actually grown up."

Many young adults envision moving out of their parents' house as a marker of adulthood, so it can feel like a step backward to move back in immediately after graduation. "The hardest thing for me was moving back in with my parents and feeling as though I had regressed," Jasmine said. "I was back in the same bedroom I lived in in high school and just overall felt like I was taking steps back."

Even though you try to establish yourself as an adult and want to make your own decisions, it can be especially difficult to not be surrounded by people your age. "Living at home was challenging for me," shared Logan. "Not because of my parents, but because of weekly boredom. All of my friends lived downtown, and I lived in a suburb. There was a lot of idle time on weekday evenings. That made me a bit stir crazy. To cope, I picked up a lot of little hobbies to keep me busy—intramural sports, new workout programs, reading."

Living at home for a period of time may come with its own benefits and challenges. If you do end up living at home, you can be comforted by the fact that you are not an outlier. The numbers do not lie: more young adults are living at home than in previous decades. Young adults are the age group most likely to live in a multigenerational home.[2] As of 2014, a record 33 percent of young adults ages twenty-five to twenty-nine lived with a parent or grandparent.[3]

There are certain times in life where you may find yourself living at home again. It could be while in between jobs or to give yourself time to look for jobs if you are unemployed. We saw how quickly COVID-19 changed this too. An analysis of government data by the real-estate website Zillow indicated that 2.9 million adults ages eighteen to twenty-nine moved in with a parent or grandparent during the first three months of the global pandemic.[4] This is the largest percentage of young adults (52 percent) living with parents since the Great Depression.[5]

Prior to 2020, the number of twenty-five- to thirty-four-year-olds living at home increased to 22 percent (between 2000 and 2017).[6] Millennials, also known as "the unluckiest generation,"[7] have experienced the slowest economic growth due to recessions in 2001, 2008, and now 2020. Between student debt and emerging into the workforce in a poor economy, it is no wonder young Americans are waiting to focus on other adulthood milestones such as marriage, buying a house, or raising kids.

Unfortunately, the future for Gen Z is looking similar. In light of these realities, it is even more important to become knowledgeable and equipped to manage your own finances.

## LIFE IS EXPENSIVE

"I don't feel prepared to start being an adult in the world," shared Jill, mainly because I feel like I can't afford it."

Both graduating seniors and recent grads face the realities of paying bills, budgeting, and taxes. Most felt woefully unprepared to manage their own finances when they left college. Even years later, we can often feel unprepared when it comes down to saving up for a down payment on a house or purchasing a car.

Many respondents to my survey expressed that they wished there was a class in school that taught students about budgeting, taxes, and finances. "School felt safe—I knew what I was supposed to be doing. Entering the real world, I felt a little overwhelmed. Insurance? Car payments? Trying to figure out what a good/livable salary is? It was a lot," Isla said. "I wished I had taken a 'life prep' course as part of the curriculum that went over filing taxes, budgets, loan payments, etc."

Jessica listed just a few of the many financial matters she felt unprepared to handle: "How to budget. How to do my own taxes. How to choose my insurance. What a 401(k) is compared to a Roth-IRA . . . It's just the logistical 'adult' things that currently our education system doesn't have a place to teach us."

Our educational systems should do a lot more to prepare us for those practical financial responsibilities, such as offering courses about budgeting, establishing credit, saving, and financial planning. Thankfully, there are resources available like financial advising and online courses, such as Dave Ramsey[8] or an online personal finance class for recent grads at Investopedia Academy[9]. Ultimately, however, earning creditworthiness, learning how to budget, and contributing to savings is best learned through personal experience.

Once starting a full-time job, you are probably making more money than you ever did previously, yet you also are responsible for paying for more than you ever did before. The basic bills include rent; cable/internet; gas/electric, heat, and water (if utilities are not included); cell phone; public transit or car insurance; auto gas and maintenance; health insurance and medical expenses; groceries; and potential student loans. Once you write out all your expenses, you realize how much it costs to live. And how little is left after paying your bills.

Even if you managed bills in college, the realities of your adult life will likely bring even more. Many graduates expressed their surprise about how many bills there were. "I've been paying most of my bills since I was eighteen," said Claire, "but post-grad I bought a car (which means maintenance, insurance, monthly payments), and have to pay off student loans, and then health insurance and 401(k) contributions and cell phones and paying for a gym membership and having a lot harder time finding events that have free pizza just for showing up."

The first tax season also provoked anxiety and fear for many graduates. I dreaded completing my taxes for the first time and delayed it for as long as possible. Once I filed my taxes, though, I felt empowered. Filing was not as complicated as I thought it would be (thanks, TurboTax), and I have felt more self-assured after doing my taxes on my own.

Budgets can be empowering when you look at your income and expenses mapped out against your own personal budget. Budgets vary person to person and will change over time depending on circumstances and job status, but it may help to get started by utilizing templates.[10]

Budgeting especially is important as you save for larger expenses. "This has been the first time I have had a real salary," said Kellan. "So, I learned how to plan my spending for things like student loans, car payments, utilities, savings, rent, food, leisure activities."

Another surprise was the difference between the gross salary and the paycheck you receive after taxes. "Money is hard to come by, and I appreciate it even more now that I am making some," Drew said. "Save up, my friends. Life is an expensive bitch."

I could not say it better myself. It is overwhelming to think about expenses, savings, 401(k)s, and taxes. However, watching yourself become financially independent can lead to increased confidence. "I would even venture to say I enjoy the real world better than college," shared Jordan. "I'm less stressed, have more free time, am making money doing what I love, live in the city I want to be in, and am taking care of myself of my own financial accord."

Financial responsibility is especially important to develop in the initial post-grad years because it builds confidence in your ability to support yourself and eventually others. The financial goals and routines you work toward after college prepare and shape your habits as you grow older. You are literally investing in your future. But financial security is not something that happens automatically. Whether you have a lot of expendable income or whether you are living paycheck to paycheck, it is important to understand budgeting, savings, and how to steward your finances.

One significant budget item for many young adults is graduating with student loan debt. Approximately 45 percent of millennials have student-loan debt[11], and the numbers only increase with age as a new study estimates that 73 percent of Gen Z students will graduate with student-loan debt.[12] The reality of student-loan debt is gravely impacting the fears of entering the workforce and the early years of our careers.

My student-loan repayment kicked in six months after graduation, and I felt the impact of this additional financial commitment. Once it was part of my monthly budget, I learned to live with it. There are options for repayment, and it is not a bad idea to get advice about the impacts of the one you choose. In the midst of the monthly payments, it is helpful to remember that you took on that debt as an investment in your education, which ultimately leads into your career.

While student loans receive a lot of attention in the media, credit-card debt can be even more crippling and may be surprisingly common. According to a study, 67 percent of millennials report having credit-card debt[13]. Based upon new research, Gen Z may be even more likely to rack up credit-card debt.[14] And with high APR rates and unforeseen expenses, it can be easier to fall into debt than you would like to admit.

Once you are there, it may feel impossible to pay it off, but start somewhere. Take a class. Become educated. Learn how to own your finances, even if that means owning your debt first. Get in the habit of paying off your credit card each month. Learn what type of budgeting works best for you and your lifestyle. Start with building an emergency savings fund to give you peace of mind in case of any unexpected costs or emergencies.

My savings saved my financial life. When I was laid off from my first job, I had managed to save three thousand dollars, which was a lot compared to my salary. Wanting to avoid depleting my savings, I focused my financial realities based upon unemployment checks. With a twelve-hundred-dollar monthly check, I was left with about three hundred dollars per month after paying rent and utilities. I paused my student-loan payments and reduced any spending where I could.

At that time, my goal was to spend no more than twenty-five to thirty dollars at the grocery store each week. A friend who had been laid off before advised not to avoid all events or outings because of how helpful it is to participate in some semblance of a social life. Taking his advice, I would occasionally join friends for a meal or drinks, but I would end up scanning the menu for the cheapest item. Living in survival mode had its mental and emotional impacts, but between unemployment checks and the safety net of my savings, I survived my first time of unemployment without going into debt.

In my first job, I was making the lowest salary of any job, and yet I transferred money over to savings regularly. It is tempting to think we can only start saving once we have a higher-paying job, but regardless of the size of the paycheck, save money. It takes intention, thought, and discipline. Saving teaches us what we can live without; it teaches self-discipline. Budgeting includes knowing when to increase saving amounts, such as when you are saving for a wedding or a down payment.

Unexpectedly, you may have costs that you could not have anticipated, whether it is a medical bill, a stolen bike, or having your car break down. Having that cushion of savings provides peace of mind for those situations and any emergencies that arise.

As we continue to see the instability of the job market and economy, savings also provides a safety net if anything happens to your income. A layoff and unemployment are stressful enough, so I personally can attest to the value of building your savings for your mental well-being. It may provide financial security when you need it most.

It is also important to ensure the pendulum does not swing the other way in having a hoarding mindset with finances. Money comes, and money goes. As I have seen in my life, it certainly helps, but it cannot be our ultimate sense of security. Your financial stability can change within minutes right before your eyes.

Giving is another component of financial health that is beneficial to yourself and those around you. Giving not only keeps us from becoming selfish with our money, but it also enables us to support causes and organizations. Millennials and Gen Zers love to participate in purpose-driven work, so we can support causes now that we earn our own income. If we have an organization we support and follow on social media, we can donate. We can use our desire to make a difference and offer financial contributions to organizations that are doing great work all over the world.

You can also have a spirit of generosity in the small things. It is always fun to treat a friend to dinner or coffee. If you are holding too tightly on to your own wallet, you will miss out on the joy it is to give.

As a financially independent adult, you quickly learn by experience how to manage your own money. Do not be afraid to ask for help. There is a lot to learn, and we will only continue to learn as we join finances with a partner or eventually raise children.

Now that you are making money, you need to learn how to manage it. Do not let it manage you.

CHAPTER 5

# HELLO, MY NAME IS . . .

### "A friend may be waiting behind a stranger's face."

MAYA ANGELOU

Our college years are a unique period in our lives. Never again will we live within close proximity to all our friends. Never again will we run into people daily in a confined campus environment. Never again will we be surrounded by hundreds or thousands of peers within a close age range.

Similar to the transition we face in our living situations and new environments, our entrance into the real world is met with a drastic change to our sense of community. Fear and sadness over leaving the community and friendships you have built over the years is normal. Your college or university was your home. It is never easy to leave a community you have built, especially when so much of your intellectual, emotional, and mental growth occurred in that environment over the years.

Reflecting on her senior year, Shannon said it was difficult to think about not having a community like it again. "There is something unique and special about living with friends and doing life with

71

all sorts of people. Yes, there will be community in the future, but not like you have in college."

Ruth felt ready to leave academically but wanted to hold on to the relationships and lifestyle of college. "I had the opportunity to be surrounded by some amazing individuals at [college] and become a part of so many diverse circles of friends who were intelligent, fun, and unique in their own way. I never had that type of social community anywhere else. It was sad to know that I would never be with those same friends in the same exact context ever again." It can feel overwhelming to have such a drastic change in community. No matter how you try to keep in touch, it will not be the same.

Mona described her unique challenges of senior year. "For me it was always leaving your best friends, your second home, a society you have become so attached to," she said. "For most international students, not knowing when the next time you will be able to recognize this different world we're leaving behind is so mentally and emotionally challenging."

Post-grad depression is common during the initial transition because of the sudden loss of community. Riley said, "I hear people talk about 'post-grad depression' and how real it is. I'm good at making friends but knowing that all my best friends will be spread throughout the country and not just down the hall is really sad and scary."

In college, we were able to see friends in classes, at meetings, or in the dorms. We could become close friends with someone in only a semester's worth of time. Now we cannot simply walk down the hall to a friend's room or across campus to an apartment to hang out. A part of the transition from college friendships to adult friendships is grieving the proximity and ease of the school structure that fostered these friendships. While those friends may remain in your life in some capacity, the context changes. Most of your college friendships will become long distance.

When I first moved to Chicago, it was not until I settled more into my life and new routines that I realized practically all my college relationships were now long distance.

Social media can be a useful tool to stay connected despite the distance or differences in time zones, as it provides an easy way to keep track of loved ones with updates, photos, and other life changes. To maintain community, we need to enhance our communication skills and put forth effort to stay in touch with people. I fail at it often—it is an ongoing challenge. It makes those times special when you see someone at a wedding, visit a friend in his city, or receive a phone call to catch up.

Lauren, a recent college graduate, believes it takes intentionality to maintain relationships. "Making time for those phone dates is so, so important and key to maintaining friendships, especially when you move to a new state."

And do not think it has been too long to reconnect. "It never matters how many days, weeks, months, or even years it's been since you've reached out to an old friend, whether it's college or high school," said Latasha. "They probably miss you as much as you miss them. It's super hard to stay in contact with everyone when we're all so busy and far away but it's so so so so important!"

Leaving behind the friends, network, and community we had in college is not easy, especially if we've moved. The challenge is to balance maintaining old relationships while simultaneously building new ones. It becomes more complex as we change jobs, move to another city, get married, or have children. For the first two decades of our lives, the structure of school set us up to make friends and build a community based on who was nearby. We did not realize how little effort we had to put into building relationships. It was provided for us. Now, it is our turn to build community for ourselves—completely on our own.

## THE END OF COMMUNITY AS WE KNEW IT

After I moved to Chicago, I soon lost track of the times I said, "Hello, my name is Cate LeSourd. I grew up in Virginia but went to school in North Carolina. I moved to Chicago recently for a job." While it was fun and exciting to meet new people, I deeply missed having those who knew me and my background.

Older friends who tried to warn us were right: "It's hard to make friends in the real world," said Cassandra. "College had clubs and teams and sororities to help you make friends that were your age, but the real world doesn't just 'present' friends to you."

The real world highlights the unfortunate reality of how difficult it is to make friends as an adult. Suddenly, we may be the only twentysomething in our workplace. In addition, we may live on our own for the first time or with random roommates and feel lonely with the lack of close friendships.

The workplace is now the adult version of school. Instead of fellow students, we have colleagues. Instead of teachers, we have managers. Instead of a classroom, we have an office. In this new structure, we can invest time and build relationships with those we see every day, but making new friends at work might be difficult if coworkers are decades older than us. While positive relationships at work are nice, we probably will not grab a drink after work or join a sports league with them.

Roseline, who worked at a nonprofit organization, said she was the youngest person in her workplace by over ten years. To make new friendships outside of work, she would have to be very intentional. "It's hard to find the time and energy to devote to building new friendships from the ground up," she said. "Relationship-building is time-consuming work, and it sometimes feels overwhelming."

Similarly, Kimberly remarked, "I'm in a profession with wonderful, caring people who happen to be fifty-five years old. Great people, great friends, but not the ones I want to hang out with every weekend."

Agency environments such as marketing, advertising, and PR typically have a younger demographic, so I was fortunate to meet people my age immediately after college. Right away, I made new friends who joined me for lunch, went to happy hours, or tried out a neighborhood festival on the weekend. My second day living in Chicago was the first day of my summer graduate internship. I walked into the office and immediately met twenty other interns in the cohort, which consisted of recent graduates, college students, and twentysomethings from all over the country. We quickly became friends and explored the city together after work and on the weekends.

That group of interns made my transition to Chicago and to my first full-time job seamless. It served as a valuable foundation of friendships that gave me confidence as I adapted to a new environment. Even though almost all of us have since changed jobs or cities since then, we still get together when we can, years later.

A cohort of some kind, whether at work or in graduate school, helps provide a way to meet peers and create a sense of camaraderie. Whether it is law school, business, social work, or any other post-grad program, those cohorts often act as a great way to meet like-minded individuals.

I met wonderful friends through my first job, but as I was settling into my new life in Chicago, I knew I also wanted to meet people outside of a work environment. My faith is important to me, so I was excited to visit different churches and become involved in a local community. I googled nondenominational churches and visited them by myself. I was not afraid to do this on my own, because I had done this the summer before in Nashville. That summer served as meaningful practice for becoming comfortable with attending events, churches, or group outings alone. Even for the most outgoing of individuals, however, it can still feel intimidating. I often walked in and out of services feeling invisible and forgettable.

I attended one church and did not think it would be the best fit for me. The next week, I attended another one. The second time I went to this church, I talked to the girl who sat next to me after the service. She introduced me to a couple of her friends, and they discussed lunch plans, but they did not invite me. Looking back, I could have asked to join, but feeling more vulnerable at the time, I said nothing and walked out by myself.

Not wanting to judge the entire church from that one morning, I decided to go back and give it another try. Ironically, I became a member of that church, and it has been my church for the entire time I have lived in Chicago. That church community became a strong sense of community in my adult life, providing me with meaningful relationships, leadership experience, and service opportunities. Looking back now, I could not be more thankful I kept going.

Connecting through a common interest helps easily build a foundation for a friendship—perhaps it is with a volunteer organization, a sports league, a musical ensemble, or a group with shared hobbies or interests.

Serena volunteered and helped children in different communities. "It helped joining an organization where I was going to be meeting a bunch of new people my age who just graduated (for the most part) also," she said. "For me it felt like the beginning of college all over again, except we were all here for one cause."

But it does not happen without effort. As recent graduate Arianna shared, "I wish I had listened to people who said you have to make an active effort to make friends after graduation. Volunteering, joining a small group at church, or participating in a recreational sports team are all great ways to meet new people. Plus, they give you something to look forward to when work weeks get monotonous."

When we go to a workout class, a bar, or a party, we can keep our head down interacting with people we know, or we can be intentional to meet others. Birthday parties or other events are a great opportunity to meet friends of friends, which can have a domino effect. Sure, you may be hesitant because you know one person at the entire party, but go for it. Put yourself out there. Be uncomfortable. It is those times that often end up creating great friendships.

"When you're trying to make new friends/put roots down/engage meaningfully wherever you are, always say yes! To everything," Jennifer suggested. "Even if you're out of your comfort zone, even if it's a challenge . . . say yes. Your community will grow and change wherever you are, but you have to start somewhere."

Starting over is uncomfortable. Be patient. It does not happen overnight. It takes time *and* effort to meet people.

"You should always put yourself out there because you never know what could happen. I met my best friend (since college) and my boyfriend at events that I almost didn't go to because I simply wasn't in the mood and was tired after work, but decided last minute that it would be worth it," Olivia said. "Now I say it's always worth it."

Adjusting to a new city and new environment takes time. It takes effort. We may not see results right away, but it will pay off.

## WAIT, SO HOW DO I MAKE FRIENDS AGAIN?

Within my first year after college, I decided to run the Chicago Marathon with a charity I supported. The cause aligned with my passion in providing communities access to clean water. I never thought I would run a marathon, but I was compelled by the opportunity to fundraise for the cause, so I hesitantly decided to sign up.

As a part of the training, I joined a fundraising team and participated in group runs on the weekends. I did not love running and was overwhelmed by the uncertainty of whether I could even run a marathon. At that time, the most I had ever run was five miles. I met others who were also running their first marathon, which helped me not feel as alone. I also got to know those in my pace group. After all, running miles and miles together results in some serious bonding.

A turning point for me was the twenty-mile training run. The organization partnered with running groups to create a trial race with a twenty-mile course laid out along the Lakefront Trail. I found my new running friends and our legs started moving. A guy named Rob joined our pace group whom I had not met before, so we talked for a couple miles. Suddenly, ten miles went by, and we were already halfway through our distance.

Once we finished the run, we went out for lunch to celebrate. Rob invited me to his birthday trolley that night and the others insisted I join them. I knew I might not have the best time, but I did not want to let that stop me from trying to make new friends. After all, every friend that you have now at some point was a stranger.

I showed up. As we bar hopped across different neighborhoods in the city, I had the opportunity to get to know these new friends better. There were moments I felt awkward not knowing others well but I walked away knowing more people and had fun in the process.

I love reflecting on this story now because some of those friends on that trolley became close friends the following year. I allowed myself to be a little uncomfortable for a night, which led to other celebrations, casual dinners, and eventually close friendships. It took ongoing effort and time to invest in those newer relationships, but it was worth it. I even gained a roommate and was a bridesmaid in her wedding years later.

Many of the friends I met through the marathon also attended the same church as me. While running a marathon together certainly bonds you in a unique way, I could easily maintain these friendships when I saw them on the weekends after the marathon was over.

Now, you do not have to run a marathon to make friends. You

can join a gym, a running club, or a sports league. And if you are not into athletic or outdoor activities at all, you can find an art class, a volunteer organization, music class, or a dance studio to try out. The goal is to find ways to meet people who share your interests and passions. Even if you enjoy spending time alone or are content with the friendships from your previous location, there is value in building new friendships where you physically live.

Everything requires intentionality, planning, and effort. It takes following up. It takes rearranging your schedule to try and find a time to get together with someone. It takes being an initiator, even if that is uncomfortable. More than likely, others will be grateful you asked them to hang out. Especially when you are new in an environment, do not be afraid to ask first.

The initial transition will be filled with countless introductions, meeting new people, and feeling homesick for old friends. Amid all these changing relationships and attempts to make new ones, you are bound to feel lonely and a bit unsure of yourself. Being the first to reach out to someone or showing up to an event alone is going to feel uncomfortable. The best thing you can do is to acknowledge that reality and choose to step into that uneasiness anyway. Pursue getting to know people—you will not regret it.

Every time you step out of your comfort zone, you are investing in new friendships. It takes time to feel settled in your new town or city, but making friends has a domino effect. Once you make one new friend, it starts to slowly build off one another as you are introduced to their friends, and suddenly, you watch an entire community unfold. And community is even more important as we navigate the challenges of our transition into adulthood.

---

## CHAPTER 6

# GROWING PAINS

"Character cannot be developed in ease
and quiet. Only through experience of trial
and suffering can the soul be strengthened,
ambition inspired, and success achieved."

HELEN KELLER

A t twenty-three years old, Lorelai was diagnosed with cancer. "The biggest challenge of my post-grad years came when I was diagnosed with Hodgkin's lymphoma nine months into my time in LA. Being forced to leave an awesome city, friends whom I loved, and independence really hurt my soul. I had to move back in with my parents, lean on others for just about everything, and focus on doctor's appointments and blood counts and chemo and whether or not I would shave my head. Things that no twenty-three-year-old should ever have to think about. Things that no one should have to think about."

"It felt like my entire life was put on hold. I had to withdraw from my soon-to-be grad program. I had to tie up loose ends with my

LA community. Meanwhile, my friends were starting jobs, getting engaged, traveling, and starting grad school."

Lorelai sought treatment, focused on her health, and eventually, she became cancer free. She was vocal about her experience on social media, which inspired all who followed her journey. While she never could have expected to be diagnosed with cancer so soon after graduating from college, she persevered through the trial. She described how her faith was her foundation and pillar of hope. Years later, she completed her master's in social work and then pursued a master's in theological studies. What could have easily held her back, propelled her forward.

A crisis may interrupt your life, test your resolve, and challenge your faith. After finishing an early-morning shift at a news station, Brandon received the shocking news that his dad was in the hospital. He was on the next flight home. He went straight to the hospital to see his father. The next day, the doctor informed the family that Brandon's father had passed away.

Gone, all in a matter of hours. Brandon described it as the hardest day of his life. "My real-life superhero and best friend was gone," he said. "Taken from me so soon. My nightmare was real."

As the days passed, Brandon slipped into a rut and did not want to do anything or talk to anyone. The shock of it all was too much to bear at times. "I tried to be strong for my family, for my mom. To lose the love of her life, I couldn't imagine what she was going through. I felt like I had to be strong. I suppressed some of my feelings. At Dad's celebration, I couldn't hold it in any longer," he said. "To see him one last time. I would give anything to see him one more time, to talk to him one more time. To tell him about so much. Sports, my life, everything."

Brandon was only twenty-three years old when his father unexpectedly passed away. While the death of our loved ones is inevitable, there is an added sense of grief when we lose a parent unexpectedly at a younger age. We grieve the loss of their life, while also grieving our future with them no longer a part of it. The grief continues.

Years later, Brandon still mourns the loss of his father, especially during more memorable life moments. "I'm getting married this June, and he won't be here," he said. "He never got to meet my fiancée. I know she would've loved him. I know he would've loved her. He would've been so thrilled to have a daughter-in-law."

Five years have passed, and he still remembers the day—the heartache and the pain he felt. In the midst of his sorrow, Brandon's faith helped keep him moving forward. "Despite all that happened, one thing has remained ever so true, and that is God is still good. He has kept me and my family since then."

Counseling helped him understand that grief is not linear; it is ongoing. During one session, his counselor said: "When you experience the loss of a loved one, you will never move on from it. You try to move forward, knowing that they will always be with you every step of the way." Brandon will continue to grieve the loss of his dad throughout his life, but he intentionally lives his life to continue the legacy his father began. The legacy of helping, encouraging, and mentoring others.

The death of a loved one is never easy. Other challenges during these transitional years force us to face circumstances we could never be prepared to handle, or even see coming.

Jaymee moved to South Africa after graduation to teach as a Fulbright scholar. After learning to drive on the other side of the road, furnishing an apartment, and finding friends and community, she slowly adjusted to living and working in a new country. And then, while traveling to the United States for a special event, she discovered she was listed as "undesirable" due to a visa incident that banned her from returning to South Africa for a year.

"I scrambled to sell my car, get out of my lease, treat a mold-infestation issue caused by a rogue roommate, and collect my belongings from South Africa, all while trapped in the US," said Jaymee. "I never had the opportunity to say proper goodbyes. To count down the days. To mourn appropriately. The life I had invested and poured myself into was ripped away in a mere matter of minutes, and I was left with the uncertain and complex jigsaw puzzle pieces to reassemble after the fallout. It felt like the worst break up I had ever experienced in my life. My breakup with South Africa."

Jaymee was left to pick up the pieces from her life abroad, which included tracing her suitcases' arrival back to the States. After battling the effects of this shocking change day by day, she eventually settled into a new life with a new job and routine. "I am happy with who I am and where I am now—I feel like a badass who can now conquer the world after all the hurdles I have needed to jump and navigate. But it took an immense amount of patience and problem solving amidst uncertain situations to reach the peak I ultimately summited. When in doubt, just keep moving."

Unexpected trials and tragedies are stark reminders that we are not in control. As much as we think we are or attempt to be, the idea of full control is an illusion. We cannot control all circumstances or the outcomes in our lives. We cannot control other people's responses, words, or actions. But we can control how we choose to respond.

When overwhelmed or discouraged, paralysis over what to do next is normal. Sometimes, the next best thing you can do may mean taking a single step forward. No one can see the full picture of our lives from beginning to end, but we can be intentional with living in the present and making decisions with the understanding we have at the time.

When we look back on past decisions, we will likely have a different perspective because of the wisdom we have gained since the time of that decision. While we wish we had more foresight, we truly only have hindsight.

The trials of life and challenges we face help us build character and resiliency. When you are on your own and responsible for yourself, you will be stretched in new ways. Knowing who you are and how to take care of yourself will have an exponential effect on your decisions, relationships, work, and life in general.

## QUESTIONING AND SELF-DOUBT

As children, we grew up in a society that provided guardrails, directing us and our decisions. The educational system mapped out the first two decades of our lives as we moved up from one grade to the next. Throughout our academic lives, we had access to a variety of teachers and professors whose focus was on teaching and guiding us to the next level of our education. Even their own career path was based sometimes on the success of their students.

Our mentors, coaches, and educators wanted to see us flourish. High-school teachers stayed after school to help us prepare for AP exams. Professors held office hours for questions. Colleges dedicated entire departments and resource centers to helping students in their internship and job search. College professors may have demanded more independence from their students, but they were still there *for* you. For your growth. For your success. For your career.

In the adult world, no one looks out for you like that. Guidance does not disappear altogether, but is increasingly difficult to find. You may have mentors, supervisors, and bosses who want you to perform at your best, but it is usually for the success or bottom line of the company. Even if you have a great mentor outside of work, you have to seek out their time and availability—it is not provided for you.

"The biggest lesson I've learned being out of college is the world really does not cater to you anymore and that you have to learn to live independently," Eliza realized. "There are no longer any school administrators, advisors, or professors whose job it is to guide you in making decisions without being asked. Now that I'm out of college, I have to seek out that guidance from mentors and older adults I admire and trust."

As students, we took for granted the access we had to mentors, teachers, and coaches. When you leave the structure of school, you leave all that behind. You are expected to make your own decisions, and you are fully responsible for any consequences of those decisions. You are in charge of your own life. No pressure, right?

"By the time most graduate with a bachelor's [degree], they have sixteen years of school under their belt. The majority of our lives," said Jaymee. "We get conditioned to a certain way of thinking, of being. We are confined within a small comfortable bubble of options and offered clear direction and parameters on how to function through course syllabi and grading rubrics. We become pros of doing exactly what our professors and leaders tell us to do."

She continues, "But life doesn't come with a handbook, manual, or grading rubric. Depending on your field of work, bosses won't necessarily write out a play-by-play of what they want you to do and when. My Fulbright fellowship and my work in the high school was fraught with uncertainty, lack of clarity, and wide-open opportunities. There were so many options, I didn't know where to begin, and I found myself floundering at first. My days of being told what to do were over. I needed to learn how to become incredibly introspective and really define who I am and where I wanted to go in life."

Without the structure of school, we are now the ones leading ourselves forward. Initially, this can lead to a lot of questioning and self-doubt.

"I didn't expect to feel so purposeless," said Arianna. "High school led to college which led to employment. However, now we get to set our own challenges. I've never felt more confused about who I am or what I want out of life than I have this year."

The combination of this freedom and responsibility is empowering and yet also terrifying. Naturally, fears coincide with our decisions and their unknown outcomes. The questions of "what if" cloud our minds. Gianna asked herself, "Was I actually qualified for my job? Could I actually make it on my own? What if I failed? What if my grades and academic success didn't translate to work success? What if I couldn't make friends? What if I hated it here and couldn't get back closer to home?"

Our decisions and thoughts can be laden with fear if we let them. We are often held back by our dread of failure. Those fears keep us from pursuing opportunities, relationships, and even dreams we have for our lives. As we get older, we may become more prone to anxiety based on prior disappointments and challenges.

While it is important to be wise and thoughtful with our decisions, we must be careful to not let our fears keep us from living well or fully in the present. "My biggest fear is and always will be, failure," said Cameron. "I don't want to waste my time. No one can tell me what's right. Life isn't a test. There's no study guide that has all the right answers written. I feel so insecure about every choice I make. Is this the right choice for me? Should I take this job? Am I dating the right person? Everything is so serious now, and I don't know how to feel confident that I'm doing what is right for me."

Although these emotions exist throughout our lives, questions and doubts rise up more strongly in times of uncertainty or change. No wonder the post-grad years are filled with immense self-doubt. We put a lot of pressure on how our decisions could impact our future. *The Defining Decade*[2] discusses our tendency for paralysis in decision-making because of internal expectations. Most decisions in our life, however, are not completely irreversible. Especially in the earlier stages of our career, we have the ability to change or pivot when needed.

Scarlett moved to New York, a place that was comfortable and familiar to her. Then she decided to apply to graduate schools abroad. Her biggest lesson? It is okay to change your mind. "Any new postgrad should be aware that it's not the end of the world if you realize that you don't want what you thought you did," she said. "What is really important is figuring out why something doesn't work out and to learn from it so you can make a better decision next time."

As much as we hate being told to learn from mistakes or decisions, it is true. All of us are going to make decisions we will probably want to change at some point. We can wallow in self-pity and regret, or we can learn from our circumstances. If we view our decisions, changes, and opportunities as learning experiences, it also frees up our mind to feel less pressure in the decision itself.

"Being an adult means making peace and honoring your life decisions," Brette advised. "You need to make choices with whatever information you can gather at the time. Sure, there will be times you wish you had chosen differently. But you can't beat yourself up about it. You need to honor who you were and what you were thinking at that exact moment in life and then move forward and live with that choice, knowing that you are growing and learning, especially when you make those "bad" decisions. In that way, no choice is ever wrong. It's just a learning opportunity that will better prepare you for the future."

Questioning may lead to redirection, a deeper sense of commitment or excitement, or even affirmation of that choice. Evaluating and analyzing options can help you gain confidence, whether continuing a path or changing directions.

Lori planned to pursue a career in higher education but started doubting herself and feared she was locking herself in. "What if I didn't like higher education? What if I couldn't make enough money? Was I setting myself up for years of graduate school without the payoff I thought I deserved? I started grasping at straws and applying for corporate jobs that didn't really make sense for my background or goals."

An interview with a financial company reminded her that she wanted to work in higher education because she appreciates the experiences that universities provide students. "If you've spent several years planning for one industry, there's probably a reason. I started panicking because I didn't immediately find something perfect and I didn't want to feel locked into one job or industry. If you get into a position and realize it's not all you hoped it would be, now you know and you can work towards finding something that will be a better fit. You are not stuck or obligated to be in that role forever. Don't freak out."

Experiencing other options may help you remember why you chose a specific field or industry in the first place. In describing her student teaching experience, Brandi said, "It opened my eyes to how life as a teacher was, and it made me question my lifelong dream of being a teacher. Questioning this made me stronger in the long run, and I am thankful to have gone through that experience."

Sam decided to travel for a year after graduation but mentioned the doubts he had before leaving. "I was nervous because I was second guessing myself. Should I go to grad school instead? Should I try to get more experience in my career? My fear was that I would lose my qualifications and skills by taking a year off to travel," he said.

Regardless of what your life looks like right now, you will probably question a decision, or several, many times. I would be more surprised if you never questioned any of your choices. Times of questioning and self-reflection can provide us with a deeper level of confidence and assurance in the decisions we make, which feels empowering.

If you worked for years towards a particular direction and want to change, you can adapt. You are not stuck. There may be consequences or realities, such as needing additional education, starting an entry-level job in a new industry, or working part time to help pay the bills, but you can accept those realities when you know why you made a decision. It is your life to steward.

"This might sound obvious," said Ethan, "but the biggest thing I learned is to take charge of my own life. Without student orgs, programs, and academic advisors, I just became a lot more responsible for getting the most out of this year. Whether it was with my job, or social life, I just realized the difference in responsibility for aspects of my own life/happiness without being in college."

It is no one else's responsibility to make decisions for you anymore. While people may offer unsolicited advice, you are responsible for yourself, your life, and your future. With that responsibility comes a sense of ownership.

As Austin realized, "Now I see that I'll need to put in effort to change the things I don't like. If I don't like a certain job, team, location—I need to be okay with changing that and not just wait for it to work itself out."

We cannot be passive with our own lives. Taking ownership over your life often involves being proactive with action or thought. We are always given a choice: to work toward changing a circumstance or work toward changing our perspective.

## SELF-REFLECTION AND PERSONAL GROWTH

In the midst of all this questioning, understanding the *why* behind a decision is key. Reflection leads to greater self-awareness, which will in turn lead to wiser, more informed decisions in the future.

In his TED Talk[3] called, "How great leaders inspire action," Simon Sinek describes how great leaders and organizations in the world all think, act, and communicate the same way. From telling stories about Apple products to the Wright brothers, he reveals how people buy into the why—the purpose—of something.

While his insights are valuable for companies and organizations, the principles can be integrated into your own personal life. Understanding *why* you are doing something will help guide you forward with purpose as you make decisions to live a meaningful life.

In asking why, you may find that your decisions may not match or look the same as someone else's trajectory. It can be tempting to compare and feel as though you need to follow a similar path, but if you know why you are doing something and it aligns with your values and career goals, you can feel confident in that direction.

Teresa remembered how her friends thought success after graduation meant moving to a big city like New York City or Los Angeles, but that was not what she wanted. "I wanted to stay in [my local community], a place that I learned to really love over my four years at [college]. I started applying to jobs in the surrounding areas and committed myself to the idea of staying local, despite the 'Why would you want to stay here?' questions."

You may not realize how much you are influenced by expectations or pressures from your close communities and society at large. It takes time to reflect and think critically about your motivations, your goals, and your current circumstances or limitations. What is best for someone else will likely be different from what is best for you.

Reflecting helps me be honest with myself and my emotions and move forward with greater self-awareness. I am an external processor and love to understand and find meaning in the small and big aspects of life. Journaling has been very helpful to my personal, spiritual, and emotional growth. Several years ago, I began writing letters to myself at the start of the new year. Each January, I review the letter that I wrote the previous year. I cannot tell you how revealing it is to read over the highlights, even the challenges, because I gain perspective as I realize what I've learned over the preceding year.

Not everyone can take time to journal or would enjoy times of reflection, but I cannot stress the importance of it enough. Invest the time in yourself to think back on your experiences and what you've learned from them. Whether it is on your birthday each year, during the new year, or on a random Thursday, take time to reflect. Set aside time to answer questions about yourself, think back on the growth over recent months or years, and make goals for where you want to be in the future.

Reflecting not only leads to interpersonal growth, but it also strengthens your interviewing skills. One of the most common interview questions is, "Tell me about yourself," and you are expected to answer fluently with concrete examples. How can you interview well if you do not know how to answer that question?

"Use this time to identify what you love and what you hate," Thomas advised. "Then continually work towards building your life around things that you love, while balancing that with always putting yourself in uncomfortable situations so you're always growing. If you don't know what makes you tick or gets you excited, you're going to have a hard time figuring out what to look for in a career."

It is worth the time, energy, and money to invest in your personal and professional development. With the pace of our lives, we are left with little time to pause and reflect. And even when we have time, we may not be left with much emotional or mental capacity to think about how our decisions influence the direction of our life. Most of us keep moving forward without asking ourselves why. Between work schedules, commitments, and relationships, days pass into weeks, weeks pass into months. If we do not step back every now and then, we can easily become stuck in routines without knowing why we're doing them or even if we're enjoying them. We may have to interrupt the momentum to change our direction or focus.

Take time to reflect on your experiences, your jobs, and your relationships. With all of the major life changes occurring within your twenties, a lot can happen in the span of a year. Many survey respondents spoke of how deeply insecure and discouraged they felt initially, only to see later how the detours acted as catalysts for where they are now.

Shelby's first year out of college is a prime example. She wanted to change degrees but felt pressure to finish in time for graduation. After she graduated, she reevaluated her life and decided to go back to school, which was difficult financially. While she was in nursing school, she worked long shifts at three different jobs to make enough money. On top of this, she was recovering from an abusive relationship.

"This past year I struggled through depression, a car crash, a bad boyfriend, and a useless degree. I thought I was in a pit of never-ending bad luck." Shelby continued, "I have a great relationship now, I'm living on my own in a new city, and I'm studying something I truly love. A year ago, I never would have imagined my life the way it is now."

"I think the most unexpected part of post-grad life for me is just the change in my sense of timing," Jessica said. "You go to high school for four years, you go to college for four years (ish), but then post-grad is indefinite. For better or for worse, we are no longer restricted by these defined periods of time, and I'm still getting used to that."

The open-endedness of the years after college can feel daunting. This new sense of timing alters our expectations for professional achievements and personal growth.

## EXPECTATIONS OF CAREER DEVELOPMENT

You knew how to navigate the school system and how to succeed in that world. However, college graduation means leaving behind a place of friendships, faculty, and mentors who know you. You enter into a new world with people who know little to nothing about you. It is exciting to have a fresh, clean slate and to build your life as an adult in a new environment. At the same time, it can be challenging to leave that college community behind.

As the president of multiple clubs and a member of countless organizations, Emily was actively involved with the student life on campus. "I felt known, and I felt important," she said. "Why would I want to leave that behind to fall back to the bottom of the food chain, to start all over as a 'nobody'? My self-worth felt wrapped up in what I perceived to be my identity in college, and I was scared to leave that behind."

As a graduating senior, you were at the top of the undergrad food chain, ready to take on the world. As a fresh graduate entering a corporate job for the first time, you become the least experienced individual in the workplace, surrounded by colleagues who know more than you do.

Those initial years after college are humbling. It takes time and patience with yourself to learn and navigate the new structure. You may feel inexperienced and yet also entitled. You may feel incompetent with all you do not know and yet frustrated because you have so much to offer that is not being utilized. Be humble and recognize that you have a lot to learn. We all do.

Millennials and Gen Zers were often told growing up that "You can do anything you set your mind to" and "You can help change the world." And yes, especially with today's emerging technology and the potential for entrepreneurship, it is an exciting time to pursue our passions. While I personally want to believe I can make a difference in this world, I also believe these internalized messages have affected our expectations of ourselves and our environment.

Higher education greatly contributes to this mindset. I heard throughout my time in college how privileged we were to pursue education and, because of that degree, how much we could offer to the world. College students are encouraged to get involved or even start clubs or organizations related to their passions. We are recognized and applauded for our engagement with the local and global community. Many programs and universities provide opportunities to serve, lead, and contribute to others in significant ways.

Whether intentionally or not, a sense of entitlement likely settled into our minds—expecting to find a great job or opportunity immediately after college. And not just a great job, but one where our unique passions and talents could help make an immediate difference. It is no wonder, therefore, we approach graduation with an urgent need to figure out our career trajectory right away or land our dream job by the time we hold our diploma. Those graduation speeches are often very moving, but their messages often create subtle expectations that you are supposed to start making a world impact the minute you walk off the stage.

"It's not a race once you graduate," said Tina. "Everyone feels pressure to have the flashiest, highest paying job right out of the gate, and the reality is that's not the norm. Don't expect the heavens to part and be granted this amazing, cushy job."

Austin agreed. "Throughout all this time you're told (by guest speakers, teachers, etc.) that your college education makes you valuable and desirable. Your colleagues and friends are off starting their own businesses, becoming social influencers, and landing big jobs with big companies," he said. "College led me to believe that I was a part of this successful and revolutionary generation—only to find out that I was only seeing the successful tip of the iceberg, and I was being placed with the rest of the class, struggling to breach the surface of success."

When you walked into the office of your first full-time job, you likely realized you were at the bottom of the food chain. That reality may be more discouraging if there was no connection to any of your passions or desires to make a difference.

Worse, if we are honest with ourselves, we probably operated under the assumption we deserved a good job. This sense of entitlement, merited or not, and the expectations it brings will inevitably crash headlong into the experience of reality. As Austin commented, "After all of this, the challenge was having to reset myself, telling myself I wasn't special, I didn't know what I was doing, and that I need to earn the respect of my peers."

It takes time to build social capital within a workplace, to understand the idiosyncrasies of team dynamics, and to determine the best way to communicate with your boss. Have patience with yourself and try to remain humble as you continue to learn.

These lessons do not disappear after your initial transition to the workplace. The learning curve is present in any new job, relationship, and environment. We are a continual work in progress, especially as we adapt and grow throughout our lives.

"Post-undergrad, I learned that there is a lot that I still have to learn," Bryan admitted. "This can be both overwhelming and frustrating. At twenty-three, it's incredibly easy to feel owed something or feel like you are underachieving. Many of us often come out of college with the idea that we will have the job of our dreams and we will climb the ladder in a couple of years' time. This is never the case. But this is okay. You are very young and you have a long journey to tackle, and it takes a strong individual to understand and appreciate this perspective."

Continually learning new skills keeps our brains stimulated. Especially in the workplace, the constant learning helps keep us engaged with the work itself, as well as with our colleagues. We are no longer working to perform on a test. We are in it for the long haul.

"Everyone is so used to being promoted after a year because that is what we did after every year in school, we went up to the next grade. I just had my one-year anniversary at work, and I still learn new stuff every day and ask questions." William continued, "I don't think anyone should be hesitant to ask questions, and you should not expect to be promoted after a year of work. You really have to earn your merit in the company."

Our expectations need to change because our system changed. We no longer live in a system that has consistent level advances after each year. We must learn what it is like to work in a way that brings results and is also sustainable for both the success of our company and for our own personal career growth. As we grow in our careers and gain meaningful experience, there is always more for us to learn. Humility and a teachable spirit will prepare us for the ups and downs we experience, particularly in the workplace.

# PART TWO

# NAVIGATING WORK AND RELATIONSHIPS

## CHAPTER 7

# RED LIGHT, GREEN LIGHT

> "If our expectations, if our fondest prayers
> and dreams, are not realized then we
> should all bear in mind that the greatest
> glory of living lies not in never falling
> but in rising every time you fall."
>
> NELSON MANDELA

The reality of adulthood includes facing the challenges and disappointments of entering the professional world. Some obstacles and circumstances, such as an unstable job market, are beyond your control. It takes grit to persevere during such times.

The rise of technology has changed jobs dramatically in recent years and will likely continue to do so in the future. Millennials and Gen Zers may get accused of job hopping, but jobs themselves are often less dependable. Staying at one company for an entire career is no longer the expectation, or even the possibility.

The millennial generation in particular has had it tough when it comes to job security. The 2008 economic downturn resulted in loss of college and retirement savings and affected the job market for the graduates entering the workforce. Many of us entered a workforce with too many graduates for too few jobs.

"I graduated college in 2008 in the middle of the worst recession since the Great Depression," said Caleb. "Any prospect of a real job after college was delusional."

"Entering the workforce as a fresh graduate in 2012, the economy was still working its way back from everything that happened in 2008," said Peter. "I graduated with wide eyes expecting that I could get any job I applied for, but it took several months for me to get an offer, and it was significantly less than what I expected it to be. But, knowing I had student loan payments about to come due, I took it."

The economy affected Julia's job search: "#recessiongrad! I decided on a career pivot late in my senior year and wound up applying for 90+ jobs in book publishing before finally landing an internship. I then worked seven days a week as an assistant/weekend nanny for my first two years in NYC."

As graduates spent their early years struggling to find work, the Great Recession cost the average millennial about 13 percent of their earnings.[2] Young adults often settled for worse jobs earlier in their careers, decreasing their lifetime earnings potential. There was a brief period of recovery before the coronavirus pandemic in 2020 rattled the economy yet again.

While millennials therefore had to face another wave of financial turmoil in their lives, Gen Z experienced this reality for the first time. In fact, a third of their jobs vaporized in two months in 2020.[3] As more Gen Z professionals enter the workforce over the next decade, they may face an eerily similar fate to that of the millennial generation.

COVID-19 dramatically impacted businesses, unemployment, and career growth. Whether furloughed, laid off, or uncertain about a company's future, many people were forced to learn how to manage anxiety and to accept the ambiguity of the job market.

As a musician, Tyler's source of income and career in the gig economy as a performer was halted. "COVID-19 has made the future completely unclear," she said. "Some days I think maybe I'll never perform again and have to find something new to do. I am still learning to focus on the next best thing rather than the end goal."

The pandemic forced many employers and professions to adapt as they were brutally impacted by city lockdowns, quarantining, and other social-distancing measures. Companies rescinded offers or initiated hiring freezes. Alissa was interviewing for a job that fell prey to such a freeze, and she struggled with the resulting uncertainty and job instability. "I was planning to make a job change that got halted due to lack of jobs during the pandemic," she said. "Not sure what I want my future career to be like—still figuring that out."

Let's face it. The economy greatly affects the health of companies, which in turn affects employment and underemployment rates and the time it takes to find work. While we hope to graduate and find a great job immediately, it is usually more difficult than we expect to find meaningful employment, or any employment at all.

"In this economy, it is more difficult than ever to find a job, and at a certain point you must stop relying on your parents for money," Laurent shared. "Many students graduate with student loans, so not making money is not an option for the large majority of graduates."

With these fears, we're seeing more college graduates beginning their careers with internships or fellowships. To save time and money, companies offer increased training or use internship programs to ensure their entry-level employees are prepared for the realities of their industry.

## THE REALITIES OF THE JOB MARKET

Americans are increasingly skeptical as to how well college actually prepares students for full-time employment. According to the Pew Research Center, only about 16 percent think a four-year degree prepares students sufficiently for a well-paying job in today's economy.[4] Even so, the majority of students choose to pursue a college education. Gen Z college-enrollment rates are even surpassing those of previous generations.[5] The path of pursuing higher education is not going away anytime soon.

Still, job opportunities in the post-grad world are impacted by the realities of the economy. The quality of the job market, or lack thereof, is a reminder of the need for patience and endurance. The process of a job search is rarely easy, regardless of when you are in it.

Katie moved to Chicago with no full-time job and started applying for opportunities. "I thought with good grades and a transferable degree (business), I would have no problem finding a job," she said. "Can't tell you how many online applications I filled out with no interviews for nine months. I was embarrassed and confused."

After finishing law school, Silas struggled with the intensity of the job search. "I wish I knew how brutal the job market could be," he said. "For the three jobs I have accepted, I have probably applied to three hundred and been formally rejected from two hundred (some don't even say no, it's just no by default). I was not prepared at first for the onslaught of nos I would get in the job market."

"Prior to starting college, I had assumed that I would be living on my own in a fulfilling full-time job right after graduation." Jessica shared, "It was very disheartening for me to be leaving college, moving back home, and returning to a position I had held prior to having a college degree."

When launching from college into the world of work, there is no assurance or promise of success. Many jobs today did not exist years ago. With social media, tech, and digital innovation, the job market and the skills required are vastly different than even two decades ago. The rapidity of innovation in technology and the impact of the economy on job availability and salaries have changed the marketplace dramatically over the last decade. With these changes, both millennial and Gen Z graduates must remain adaptable, letting go the misconception of a traditional path.

How quickly jobs changed and evolved during the realities of the COVID-19 pandemic. New ways of conducting businesses forced adaptation, especially with collaboration and communication. Thankfully, technology and applications provided the necessary tools to make many jobs function remotely. In other cases, opportunities arose during this time because of a clear need. In the Age of Innovation, we will continue to see an influx of ideas and new technologies.

Many of our parents and grandparents worked at the same company or in the same profession for decades. Today, such a career path can limit mobility, opportunities, and career growth.

"There was once a time where you worked and you didn't complain. The hours were long, and the reward was little. But this isn't 1950 anymore," observed Derek. "The internet is the Wild West of consumerism. It's given us the power to change things—to do what we love. But like the West, it's still dangerous and risky to travel out there."

Our generation's ease and familiarity with technology empowers us to start our own projects or even our own businesses. We understand the power of influencers on social media and can market ourselves and our ideas. Many of us freelance or have a side hustle, which gives us the freedom and flexibility to do what we love. We are not afraid to create our own work.

In recent years, millennials have transformed the workforce. In 2016, they became the largest generation in the US labor force.[6] By 2022, Generation Z will make up a quarter of the workforce.[7] To attract and retain talent, companies are finding they must adapt to the different desires and goals of millennials and Gen Zers. These large younger generations have disrupted the job market and the culture of work itself.

Millennials place an emphasis on corporate social responsibility, have reverence for the environment, value experiences over material things, and are proficient in building communities around shared interests.[8] Both millennial and Gen Z graduates prioritize salary and work-life balance as key factors when considering changing jobs. Gen Z, however, places more value on job duties whereas millennials desire career-growth opportunities.[9] Gen Z employees want to know their role itself has meaning.

Both millennials and Gen Z desire purpose-driven work that can be enjoyed. As author and social justice leader Howard Thurman famously said, "Don't ask what the world needs. Ask what makes you come alive and go do it. Because what the world needs is people who have come alive."[10]

We want our jobs to bring a sense of purpose rather than just a paycheck. We want to care about our work. We want to work for and buy products from companies that share our values. Gen Z increasingly supports companies that share in values of doing good. To adapt to Gen Z as they increase in the workplace, companies and employers will need to highlight their involvement as global citizens and their commitment to societal challenges.[11]

By attaching so much meaning to our work, our identity is often wrapped up in our careers. We may not even realize how much we associate our sense of self-worth and confidence in relation to our career, salary, or job title.

We first experienced this on college campuses. One of the first questions anyone will ask is, "So, what are you majoring in?" Our answers automatically result in assumptions, associations, and opinions in the mind of the one who asked. The same is true in the real world when we ask, "So, what do you do for work?" Often, your answer defines you. In just seconds, your words infer who you are.

In our twenties, much of our identity is wrapped up in what we do—our career paths, our jobs, our accomplishments. And while these are good aspects in and of themselves, we have to be careful not to derive our entire sense of identity from our jobs or careers.

"We live in a culture that is all about us and self-gratification. We don't have to *love* our job all the time—that isn't reality," cautioned Rebecca. "Find something you're gifted at and do it. I've learned that we can't seek to find our identity in our job and career and that when we do that, we will fail and it will fail us."

Demanding high expectations of our professions to fulfill this need for meaning and purpose leaves us disillusioned when a job fails to deliver on those expectations. It is perhaps in these times, when the desire for meaningful work clashes with the realities of our experiences, that we find ourselves growing the most.

While some may have found a great job that aligns with long-term plans immediately after college, the questionnaire responses revealed this was not the norm. Our career paths are usually not direct but consist of twists and turns, unmet expectations, and life pivots. How we respond to these delays and disappointments is not only a significant part of our career development, but also key to our personal development.

## DEALING WITH REJECTION

Graduating college without a job lined up is common. In fact, about 53 percent of recent graduates are unemployed or underemployed, and the average college graduate needs about three to six months to find their first employment.[12] Even with a strong résumé, meaningful references, and relevant internship experience, having a job offer in hand by the time you walked across the graduation stage is the exception rather than the rule. We spend our entire academic careers preparing for the moment when we launch into our first job, often to be met with disappointment for how long it takes to find one. Comfort can be found knowing you are not the only one who is facing the difficulty of finding a job. "I really didn't expect to see how many of my peers/twenty-somethings were also struggling in some ways to find a career and become financially independent," Jessica said. "I took some comfort in the fact that others in my graduating class were also working jobs they were overqualified for and facing similar obstacles in the job search."

During our initial job search or even after, we may find ourselves working at a minimum-wage job trying to make ends meet. Dominique said, "I wasn't able to land a full-time job in my chosen career at first, so I worked at a restaurant and took an internship for my first year out." While discouraging at the time, that internship gave her valuable work experience, which later resulted in a job offer.

Finding a job can be difficult because many entry-level jobs now require having one to two years of experience. It is discouraging to apply for jobs to gain experience, only to be told you need experience. This phenomenon is commonly referred to as the entry-level catch-22.[13]

"I didn't expect to feel I'd taken a step back," said Powell. "I thought, *I have a college degree! Isn't that enough to get me in the door at these jobs?*"

Heidi described her own experience with the entry-level catch-22. "I didn't have any great internships to speak about—I supported myself in college and waitressed/bartended, so I was never in a situation where I could take an unpaid or minimum-wage internship and get by," she said.

At times, the workforce can seem impossible to break into. Securing that first job may feel like an insurmountable task. When the job market has more candidates than it has jobs, there is a strong applicant pool. Companies are forced to navigate those deep waters, which leads to an influx of internship programs. Post-grad internships *are* the new entry-level job.

Additionally, fellowships and gap programs appeal as a way to avoid the abyss of job uncertainty, offer work experience, and provide structure in life post-graduation. Those programs typically offer a plan for the first year or two after college, which can be a relief in the midst of disappointments and uncertainty.

"This was frustrating to my parents and my friends' parents; they had the assumption that college should be making you hirable," said Allison. "I think this is a right assumption. I think there is a gap between what college is teaching and what employers are looking for."

Before graduating college, your résumé is defined by leadership in organizations, part-time work, and summer internships. Once you graduate, however, you are immersed in the job market and might need to consider an internship to get your foot in the door. If you accept an internship position after college, it will be discouraging to not have a full-time job, but an internship can often lead to a full-time offer. Internship programs are competitive because companies use them as a talent pipeline, especially for their junior-level talent. It is less risky for a company to hire an intern who has already settled into the work culture and built rapport with the team. An internship or a contractual or temp-to-hire role allows both the candidate and company to determine whether the job is a good fit.

Applying for your first job has enough stress of its own. On top of that, an entire graduating class from schools across the country is trying to enter the job market at the same time. Each year, about two million students graduate college and enter the workforce.[14] Normally, professionals look for new hiring opportunities at various times throughout the year. When you graduate, however, you're competing for these entry-level jobs against the largest candidate pool you will ever face.

As a Communications major, Kathleen knew not to expect to find a job right away, but she worked hard during her job search. "Most of my friends found stuff right away, and it took me seven months," she said. "When I moved here, I was told by alums that I'd most likely have something by the end of the summer, so when that didn't happen, I got super discouraged. It was a grueling process for sure, especially living in a competitive city like New York."

Marcus, too, felt the dilemma of the entry-level catch-22. "I searched every day for about five months, and I had great interviews and opportunities, but they always chose someone with more experience," he explained. "I was shocked at how hard it was to find a job." Thankfully, he suddenly received three offers in a span of one week and decided on his first job. Timing is everything.

Watching peers work while you are still searching and interviewing can add to the sense of failure. You are witnessing someone else live the life you're trying so hard to create for yourself. "It's so easy to compare yourself to your friends because you think, *We've been together for four years, we're all on the same track, same timeline.* But you're not. Industries have different timelines for hiring, people have different skills, availability varies widely," explained Lori. "Don't feel defeated when your friends already have jobs."

For some graduates, location also plays a large role in the job search. It is hard to apply for jobs when you do not live near them. For others, location is irrelevant, or completely unknown. As a journalist, Meredith knew exactly what positions to apply for, but the location was up in the air. She said, "I was confident I would have a job. Where? I didn't know. I knew the 'what' but not the 'where.'"

Rejection inevitably comes with the interview and job search process. Christopher remembered his first disappointing year out of college. With experience in three journalism organizations, five internships, and many extra-curricular activities, he thought he was set. The role he applied for would only be offered to one recent graduate a year. "After months of waiting, multiple writing tests and interviews, phone calls and hours of studying their work, I woke up to the news that I could not believe. I got runner-up for the position, which means everything was for nothing," Christopher said. "I was so sure I'd get that position . . . that I really didn't have any backups prepared."

Because he needed to pay bills, he got a part-time job at a pizza shop. It was a humbling experience, but the disappointment gave him time to reflect on whether he wanted to continue in the direction he was heading. "What's funny is that I never intended to be a 'journalist.' I just found a way to turn my love of reading history/news into a possible livelihood," he said. After not being under the same pressures he once felt, he realized he wanted to focus on pursuing music. "Honestly, it's something I'd always wanted to do, but it took a 'push' to get me to go in that direction."

Closed doors often act as a catalyst for change. Disappointments can redirect our paths if we do not let rejection keep us from moving forward.

Katherine expressed how each rejection sent her into a spiral, questioning why she was passed over and trying to figure out why she was not selected. In time, she realized that she does not see the background of what happens on the other side. "You could have not gotten that job because another candidate may have had a connection, or that they went to the same college as the hiring manager," she said. "Accepting that truth, that you don't know what you don't know, saved me when I was job hunting initially."

Tyler applied to over one hundred jobs and heard mostly nothing except for a dozen automated rejection emails. "That was pretty brutal," he said. "Eventually, I made peace with the fact that I was going to have to move to the city I wanted to live in first then get a job." He learned that for his field of expertise, he needed to move to the city to have more application opportunities. He learned a lot about what to include or remove from a résumé and how to cater an application or cover letter for a specific company.

The disappointments grow, the discouragement deepens, and the anxiety becomes crippling. The more nos you receive, the more difficult it is to hope for that yes. The sting of rejection may threaten your view of yourself and your confidence. Do not let intense emotions and current circumstances dictate your sense of worth or value. Our brains are hardwired to pay more attention to negative events, which leads to a negativity bias and explains why we often overthink a job rejection.[15]

Rejections are an unfortunate part of the application process. We need to process the disappointment, but we cannot let it alter our view of ourselves, especially when unemployed. "Your employment status does not define who you are, what you're capable of, or the value you can offer to a company," said Michael.

In these times, perspective shapes how we view our circumstances. The specialized staffing agency Robert Half provides recommendations for how to recover from a job rejection, including focusing on strengths, staying positive, and maintaining momentum.[16]

Take advantage of learning opportunities. For instance, you might revise your strategy based on feedback from the interviewer, ask a mentor to schedule a mock interview, or request informational interviews to strengthen your professional network.[17] Another tactical approach to work through rejection is to write down your accomplishments so you have ready examples to convey your experience and skills with more confidence.

The experience of job searching can parallel to dating. As Brette said, "The job search is the worst. It's like a terrible online dating game where you put yourself out there online, writing dozens of personalized cover letters to catch the eye of 'the one.' If they like you, they ask you out on a first 'date.' If they really like you, they ask you out for a second 'date.' You get vulnerable, share your life story, try to convince them of how great you really are . . . and then you never hear from them again. Or they tell you 'You were great, but I chose someone else.' It's like getting to the final rose ceremony of *The Bachelor* and then being the one who is sent home bawling in a limo."

It took Brette two months of searching full time while unemployed to land a job she wanted. "During that time, I was offered a job, and it was rescinded three days later. I was a finalist on four different occasions and then told they chose the other person. Stay persistent. Stay determined. And believe in yourself. Something will work out eventually."

Similarly, Jake said, "Don't be afraid to date a couple companies. Figuratively, of course. Just as we literally date to better understand what type of person we'd like to spend the rest of our lives with, so is the case with unemployment. A career is a lifelong thing. And the economy and job market 'allow for' job dating. There is wisdom and value in planting your feet with longevity as well, but the first few years when you're just figuring out 'what' you even want to be doing . . . don't be afraid to date."

With that mentality, you can let go the expectation that your first—or any—job has to be perfect. This will give you a sense of freedom to explore and learn what kind of role and environment works best for you.

The job search tests your resilience and perseverance. Even if you get rejection after rejection, do not give up. Keep moving forward. Continue to network, apply, and interview.

## DIFFERENT PATHS

A job offer does not mean you have to accept it. There are times and reasons to turn it down, depending on different factors.

After graduating, Stephanie had multiple pathways in front of her. "I had two job offers that paid $55K a year, [an offer] that any recent grad would dream of," she said. "Although the companies were great, the work I would be doing wouldn't be meaningful to me. It was an incredibly soul-searching process of figuring out if I should begin my life after graduation knowing that I wouldn't be able to pay off that debt for a long time if I decided to take a year of a service job. On the other hand, I could pay off the debt shortly if I took a job that would make me unhappy for now, but which would provide flexibility to do more in a few years once the debt was paid off."

Stephanie decided to take the year-of-service position. Although she lived paycheck to paycheck, she did not regret her choice. "The experience was exactly what I wanted in terms of finding meaning in my work and engaging in community. I think a year of loving what I did set me up for better opportunities once my fellowship ended. My next step is a fantastic graduate program, and I know I would have never had this opportunity if I hadn't taken the risk of a year-of-service."

Millennials like Stephanie are often willing to take a pay cut in order to pursue a purpose-driven career. Her story also shows how difficult it is to make a decision that could provoke judgment from others. Many people would have been thrilled with either one of the offers and taken the job, no questions asked. Stephanie, on the other hand, needed to decide what she ultimately wanted out of her career. She evaluated the opportunity based on her values and dared to choose a different path that would help her reach those career goals.

Taking a pay cut is not a foreign concept for both millennial and Gen Z graduates. A study found that millennials would take an average pay cut of $7,600 if they could improve their career development, find more purposeful work, have a better work-life balance, or enjoy a strong company culture.[18] Similarly, a study found that for Gen Z, empowering work culture is two times more important than higher salary for employee retention.[19]

There is more to a job than its salary; however, it is important to evaluate the salary in light of the other elements of a job. Taking a pay cut may occur at the beginning of your career or years later. Perhaps you will take a pay cut for a specific purpose, such as aligning your job with your values or goals. As a physical therapist, Lily described an accomplishment she was proud of: "Opting for a lower-paying job to work with a population I love and to provide more stability in my life." Clearly, salary is not everything.

Not everyone will pursue a career in the corporate world. You may live a different lifestyle, work a different routine, or pursue a path in the creative arts. Still, even if you are passionate about your path, you can wrestle with the societal pressures and comparison to your peers.

Naseem felt the pressure of living in Silicon Valley but not working in tech. "I wish I knew when I graduated that it would be okay not to go down the regular path of joining the tech world like we're so accustomed to in the Bay Area," she said. "I felt like I had to land a job at Google, Apple, or Facebook and if not, then I wasn't adequate enough." Naseem overcame her insecurities and ended up starting her own successful event-planning company.

Leaving behind a structured job to pursue your own business is risky. Emily was one who took that risk. "I am most proud that I took the scary leap to start my own businesses as a freelancer," she said. "I took the opportunity and made the most of it, so now it is my full-time gig." What once felt overwhelming as a possibility for Emily now proved to be a viable source of income.

Self-employment is another beast. Courtney learned a lot about managing her own business, time, and expectations as a wedding photographer. "When I was first starting my business, my turnaround time was incredibly quick (and it also stressed me out like no other)," she said. "I've learned to give myself time to edit and not put pressure on myself to turn around at a rapid speed. I've also learned that clients value the hard work and time I put into their photos/films!"

Tanner moved to Los Angeles to pursue his dream of being a feature-film cinematographer. As he freelanced in LA, he quickly learned that he did not want to continue pursuing that dream. This was a tough realization because up until that point, he'd focused his entire career towards that goal.

Eventually, he and a friend started their own film company. Managing their own business quickly taught them how to say no to projects that did not fit their vision. "The power of no has led me to create a niche for myself, which in turn led me to create a strong mission for my new company," Tanner said. "People approach us already wanting the style we've set for ourselves. It leaves room for what matters to us and makes our job worthwhile and purpose-driven."

Working for yourself or working as a freelancer for a larger organization provides an opportunity to use your skills to serve clients with short-term projects. Within three years of graduating, Jason, a freelancer in production, had worked a total of five jobs, two short-term temp jobs, and a couple of additional projects. "I've met a ton of people, have a lot of connections all over the place, and learned a lot of different things," he said. "I've never gotten bored or complacent anywhere. It works for me!"

Freelancing provides targeted opportunities and specific growth; however, it is often not the most reliable. Joey moved to LA with a seasonal contract at a sports network, which led to an atypical freelance lifestyle. For half of the year, he had a steady paycheck and worked five days a week. For the other half of the year, he was left to fend for himself.

"It's scary but exciting to see if you can (a) make it and (b) use that time to pursue other interests and passions. For instance, the first offseason I worked for a different network, in a different sport, in a different city. It was more focused on live daily television as opposed to the work I did for the weekly show previously. While it was still a seasonal contract, it taught me new things and honed different skills, and I'm ultimately a better producer because of it," Joey said. "It's a fun albeit scary lifestyle, and while I certainly don't want to be freelance for the rest of my life, I do enjoy it for this period of my life."

Not everyone is made to follow or will even thrive in structured, corporate environments. If your career looks different but aligns with your goals and aspirations, embrace it.

Conor initially began his post-grad years as a teacher, but it exacerbated his anxious and perfectionist tendencies. After then working in marketing, he had to deal with layoffs. During this time, he became a group fitness instructor on the side and continued working classes part time.

"I thrived in that job, and they offered me full-time, so I left my marketing job to do that," Conor said. "It was hard because I've always wanted to climb some sort of ladder, so jumping off the marketing ladder was tough."

Conor's story shows why it is important to take time to identify your strengths and your own career aspirations. It takes courage to change directions, especially when it is different from what you anticipated or expected. However, when you are aware of your goals, you can make better decisions that align with who you are—your values and your beliefs—with confidence.

# BARRIERS TO ENTRY

"Without continual growth and progress,
such words as improvement, achievement,
and success have no meaning."

BENJAMIN FRANKLIN

After two decades of education, you have finally finished . . . only to pursue more education.

Additional training or higher education may be required in order to practice or engage in certain careers. If you enter graduate school straight from undergrad, you prepare all throughout your senior year for the process. You may delay the transition from student to professional, but you now have to focus on one field or profession.

Going to graduate school can be a great way to pivot or change. Evie graduated with a major in journalism and initially applied for entry-level roles but then adapted her plans to earn a master's and doctorate to become a professor. "I couldn't see myself being a journalist when I was graduating, but I thought it was what I had to do," she said. "Now I can see myself being a professor, and it feels so much better than trying to force myself to go down the path I was 'supposed to.'" Graduate programs can offer you flexibility to change directions or help you pivot into a different career path entirely.

Pursuing further education takes mental stamina. Going straight into another program after undergraduate may help keep the momentum and normal routine of studying for exams and writing papers. Others may take time off or gain work experience first, which is also beneficial.

Before preparing for medical school, Mason took a year off and worked at a job that provided invaluable experience for him. "I wish I had known that taking off that year between undergrad and grad school was actually really, really good for me. I was apprehensive about it, but it was so restful, it allowed me to hit med school with a running start and a fresh mind."

Whenever you begin a graduate program, you enter a field of study to gain a more specialized education and level of expertise. While meaningful, the workload will be more difficult than undergraduate work.

"The most challenging part about this year was the academics," said Anna. "I was thankful to meet the most amazing and supportive people in my program who have made the challenging coursework more manageable. Although it was stressful, it is rewarding to know that I am one step closer to becoming a nurse practitioner."

Pierre described the hardest part of post-grad for him: the workload. "Law school is freaking hard," he said. "The hardest I've worked in my life. So much studying."

If you have entered a prestigious program, you may feel intimidated being surrounded by others who are as passionate and excited as you. "I had a terrible case of 'imposter syndrome.' I was heading to an Ivy League institution for grad school. Who, me? I do not belong there. I'm not smart enough to be part of this program. My peers won't respect me," Valerie said. "I admit, I still have 'imposter syndrome' even when I tell people that I am an alumna."

"I was worried that maybe [my college] had not been challenging enough and that I would be 'exposed' once I got to [law school] as much lesser than everyone else," Silas admitted.

Imposter syndrome is very common—and not just in grad programs. The insecurities can be particularly strong in newer environments. In these moments, remember you were accepted into the program or job for a reason. Clearly, the admissions office or hiring manager thought you had potential. Do not let doubts creep in to make you think otherwise.

The competitive nature of these programs is another barrier. When Garrett applied to business schools, he thought he was a strong candidate for an MBA. "I applied in two separate years, so to be rejected twice was really difficult," he said. "That had been an end goal for me as I thought about my early career, so it took a lot to reorient my career goals and what I wanted out of life."

Kimberly remembered the difficulty in gaining entry into graduate school. "My plan was to go to grad school, but I was waitlisted at the two schools I applied to and didn't know where to go from there."

Not all applications will end in acceptances and set plans. For some, rejection may force plans to be reconsidered and serve as an opportunity to evaluate a need to pivot, adapt, or try again.

As with first jobs, the divergent path within graduate school can be disappointing. Renee struggled with the internship that was a required aspect of her program. "I was given a field placement assignment as part of my curriculum required for school that brought a lot of confusion, depression, and upset feelings to the year," Renee said. "What I did three days a week for my year (an unpaid required internship, essentially) was the most out of touch I've ever felt from my personal purpose of wanting to impact, serve, and heal others."

She said she "had high expectations of a master's program being the premiere setting to learn and practice social work. More so, I didn't expect the level and magnitude of how much self-reflection and introspection would happen, as well as having to spend so much time alone." Part of what helped her through this first year was to let go of specific expectations for how things would unfold and to practice self-care, which resulted in a better experience during the second year of her program.

Graduate programs help sharpen skills and also provide direction for those who initially lacked clarity on how to pursue their specific interests. After graduating college, Audrey moved to Ecuador to work as a teacher with children and families. In time, she realized she wanted to apply that passion toward immigration policy work. "I've been interested in US immigration issues for a while," Audrey said, "but I didn't realize how universal immigrant/refugee/asylee issues were until I saw the effects of the Venezuelan political crisis in Ecuador."

She described observing "how the barriers Venezuelans faced in Quito were rooted in issues like xenophobia and legal status that could be addressed with better policies. Meanwhile, in the US, the immigration debate was only becoming more contentious and harmful to newcomers. That's when I decided to go to grad school and study public policy." Audrey allowed her passions and interests to direct her towards a field of study.

"I'm really glad I went back to school," she continued. "Even though it meant giving up a very stable, comfortable life abroad. Grad school has allowed me to explore my passions and refine my skills, since I came out of undergrad with such a broad set of soft skills and interests."

Advanced degrees can open up opportunities and provide other benefits within a career. Maeve studied human services in undergrad and knew she wanted to pursue higher education to become a licensed social worker. "I am so proud of getting my master's and an advanced clinical practices certificate after that." After reaching her goal of getting an LICSW, Maeve has practiced independently and received a pay increase.

Graduate school is a specific way to further develop skills and interests as it relates to a particular career path. For many careers, however, the preparation does not end with school. Once you finish the program, you need to pass an exam or gain certification before you can practice or work within that field. The preparation continues.

## EXAMS STILL EXIST

After finishing an undergraduate or graduate degree, most celebrate the fact that they never have to take a test again. School is over. Forever.

However, that is not the reality for everyone. Depending on the career or industry, there may be assessments, certifications, or board exams to qualify for certain jobs. In order to practice certain professions, you will have to first pass those exams.

When Kiara graduated from college with her nursing degree, she struggled passing the NCLEX. "It was frustrating at the time because I just wanted to be a nurse but had to pass the test first," she said. "I spent hours studying every day while I watched a lot of my friends move on to nursing jobs. I spent a year studying for the boards and finally passed the third time."

Many nursing graduates take prep courses after graduating to prepare for this daunting task. The pass rates, according to the NCSBN, are cut in half after one attempt.[2] On top of that, each exam attempt has a financial cost, so students feel the pressure of passing the first time for the sake of their time and money.

While open-ended timelines for tests allows for flexibility, your peers may hear their results before you even take the exam. Raquel took multiple prep courses to prepare for the NCLEX. As she continued studying, she saw others with whom she graduated share their success stories on social media. "It was equal parts exciting and disheartening. Would I be one of them soon?" After taking the test, she anxiously awaited the results. "I logged in and as the page loaded, I scanned for the words that would indicate my pass or failure. Then I saw it. The word 'passed.'"

Studying for an exam and waiting for results can reignite insecurities and self-doubt. Joanna spent months studying for the PANCE, the certification exam to become a Physician Assistant. She initially enjoyed having dedicated time to study but quickly refocused her mindset on her preparation. "I had to let go of my goal of mastering each and every piece of material. There would be things I didn't know, but hey, I only needed to get a 65 percent to pass. So, while I still studied as much as I could, the most important mind change I had was letting go of perfection, being okay with some healthy anxiety, and trusting the two years of hard work I had done leading up to that time."

This requires a major shift in mindset—the goal used to be studying to score the highest number possible on an exam. Now, the goal is to pass. The exam is what enables you to practice your career, but it is not your career on its own. You have years ahead to learn and grow through hands-on experience.

Exams may be an entry point into a career or a way to level up in your career, but we are no longer graded as we were in school. As Sabrina reflected, "In school, we strive for the A. We want the 100. If you're competitive like me, you want to set the curve and be the best in the class. Although there is nothing wrong with that, it's just not likely going to happen in the real world. All you need is a 75 . . . Passing is passing."

This time of studying is part of the transition from being a student to becoming a professional. Part of your new identity includes the letters or qualifications that will be added after your name. The exam not only enables you to practice a profession, but it also certifies you as a specific professional.

With the National Physical Therapy Board Exam looming over her head, Lily spent months studying. "The morning of the exam I was all jitters. It was a beast. The mental block I experienced during that test was unprecedented in my world," she said. "Normally a moderately fast test taker, I sat for almost the entire five-hour test period. I changed answers, my eyes got fuzzy, my brain overanalyzed everything. I walked out confident I had failed."

Then she discovered she passed. "I was officially Lily, PT, DPT. And so that chapter of my life closed, and a new one called 'job hunt' had begun." Once the stress of passing an exam subsides, it is quickly replaced with the stress of finding a job within that profession. The uncertainty continues.

Law school is another example of this reality. After spending three years in the graduate program, a single exam determines whether or not you can practice law. Studying in law school and studying for the bar are different processes, and often people find that the program does not prepare you to take the exam. Many students gave up short-term jobs they enjoyed in order to focus on preparing for the exam. Studying for the bar is a full-time job.

In most jurisdictions, the bar exam is offered only two times a year.[3] Since you cannot start your career until you pass, the pressure is intensified knowing you have limited opportunities to succeed. Once you finally take the bar exam, the results will not be released until months later.

"The whole time you just think to yourself that you are actually waiting for your life to begin," Reagan said. "Either you are waiting to take the test again or you are waiting to get sworn into the bar and waiting to find a full-time job."

Reagan did not pass the bar the first time. Disappointed, she entered another intense period of studying. She took the exam a second time, followed by more waiting. Months later, she learned she had passed.

"I think what I've realized through all of this is that life is a bunch of different seasons of waiting disguised as other things. Which isn't actually as bad as it sounds. It's how you handle the times of waiting and what you do with that free time that defines you," said Reagan.

The process of studying prepares you not only for the examination but also for the realities of the world. Your knowledge is tested with the exam questions, but your discipline and determination are tested as you await results, deal with rejection, and persevere with grit. You may forget test answers, but the lessons and character developed during this time stay with you in adulthood.

Sean, an accountant, felt the pressure of needing to pass all four CPA exams within one year. "I'd argue that these tests (whether it be the CPA exam, LSAT or BAR, MCAT, Boards, etc.) are just as much a test of yourself—your endurance, patience, self-control, discipline, and emotional strength—as they are a test of the material. And you will no doubt be a stronger person because of it."

Preparing for and taking these exams requires sheer determination and discipline. The true test is what you do in response to studying obstacles, failed exams, or other challenges.

Connor decided to embark on becoming a Chartered Financial Analyst, which is one of the highest distinctions in the investment management profession. According to the CFA Institute, a typical candidate takes four to five years to pass all three exams, studying on average at least three hundred hours for each level.[4] Securing the CFA is no small commitment.

After studying for six months, Connor took the Level I exam and waited for an additional two months to find out whether or not he passed. Soon after he found out the results that he passed, the study cycle began again to prepare for Level II.

"At the time of me writing this, I am less than two months away from taking the Level II exam [for the CFA]. Despite the fact that I've been studying for about six months, I am still always anxious that I won't be prepared. The exam is constantly on my mind, and I have to make sacrifices almost every day to make sure that I'm putting in the adequate time that's required," he said. "It's truly a little frightening and depressing that you might put so much time and effort into something that you will probably fail (the average passing rate is around 43 percent each test)."

Subsequently, he discovered he had failed the exam. He'd spent months preparing for it, taking practice tests, and saying no to activities in order to study—all to end up not passing.

"The idea of potentially having 'nothing' to show for my hard work was very discouraging and stressful," he admitted. "I couldn't stop these thoughts from frequently entering my mind and even causing me to question whether I should be in the finance industry at all."

Amidst the questioning and discouragement, he continued forward and prepared to take the Level II exam a second time. He displayed a strong amount of determination, discipline, and faith to combat the disappointing realities of studying again.

In her book *Grit: The Power of Passion and Perseverance*, professor, researcher, and author Angela Duckworth writes the secret to achievement is not talent but a blend of passion and persistence, otherwise known as grit. She shares how success and accomplishment were often tied to how one kept moving forward after failure.[5]

Despite the obstacles of failing the Level II exam, Connor persevered. After another year of studying and preparing, he passed Level II. And eventually, he passed Level III and officially earned the CFA designation. Through it all, he had grit.

For those of you who needed to pass certain qualifications, you know the sense of relief and accomplishment at seeing the word *Passed*. What was once an obstacle to begin your career is now a milestone you achieved.

"When I finally got my results, it was such a relief! Much more satisfying than graduating," said Joanna, who became a Physician Assistant. "Also, a crazy amount of excitement to be finally done with studying and eventually start the job I had been working toward for ten years!"

Studying for these certifications, boards, or examinations will be draining. Whenever you find yourself overwhelmed or discouraged, remember to focus on the reason why you are taking the test.

These times of preparation for your career lead to refined passion and increased determination. The hours you spend preparing and learning will eventually pay off, even if it is in a different way or timeframe than you expected.

Regardless of how or when you start your career, it will require perseverance, hard work, and a bit of hope. The different tracks enhance your character development as you prepare to begin your career. Whether pursuing a nontraditional route, finishing a graduate program, or passing a certification exam, it is time to face the realities in the working world.

## CHAPTER 9

# THE END OF PARTICIPATION TROPHIES

**"Great companies don't hire skilled people and motivate them, they hire already motivated people and inspire them."**

SIMON SINEK

The job search, no matter how old you are, can be difficult and downright exhausting. Self-doubt and insecurity can spiral out of control. When you start a new job, acknowledge that a company decided you were qualified and offered you the position. Walk into the office or workspace on your first day remembering that you are knowledgeable, skilled, and qualified.

"At that moment I thought—wow!" Felicia remembered. "They are actually going to pay me to do something I love; I must be prepared! Though it is hard to really admit that I didn't feel prepared until someone basically told me I was, I think this is true for so many of us college graduates. We have been in a sheltered environment for so long, so when you are put in a sink-or-swim situation and you swim, you are actually shocked and think *Oh, right, I've been taking swimming lessons for four years now!*"

Just as you learned how to succeed in school environments, you must now learn how to navigate, even succeed in your professional environment. Early in your career, learn how to seek, receive, and respond to feedback. Those lessons help us throughout the entirety of our careers.

## FEEDBACK AND EVALUATION

After two decades of structuring our lives and performance around school and its expectations, we now must fit in with the rest of the working world. We have to adjust to an entirely different structure, one that can create frustration and anxiety.

The structure of school provided us with constant, immediate feedback through grades, tests, papers, rubrics, and other forms of assessments. If we wanted a good grade, we would follow the rubric guidelines for an assignment. If we were close to failing a class, it was not a shock. If we aced a test, we quickly received that affirmation. From gold stickers to the Dean's List, we gained recognition if we did well. For two decades, we relied upon this continual assessment and affirmation.

We may not realize how much we took feedback for granted until we no longer have it.

Becca was an academically minded student, heavily involved in extracurricular activities. Only years later did she realize how much she had relied on assessments and the external affirmation to shape her self-image. "My biggest challenge has been wrestling with self-doubt and a lack of confidence in my own abilities. I was not aware of how much I fed off of the validation I received as a student (grades, awards, etc.) and how much my self-worth hinged on that encouragement. I have been working on redefining my worth and recognizing my own value, but this is a process and a daily battle."

If you were an athlete, you knew if you were doing well based on your athletic performance and feedback received from coaches. You knew when you missed the shot. You knew when you fumbled the ball. You knew when you dropped the baton. Even scoreboards informed you and the crowd how you were performing.

The real world, however, does not provide constant feedback, coaching, or affirmation. Sure, there are annual performance reviews. But you adjust from constantly knowing where you stand to the uncertainty of not knowing how you are performing.

"In school, the whole point was to get good grades so you could move onto the next grade and continue this never-ending cycle of education," Mark reflected. "But facing the real world, I didn't know how to measure my success or even if I was supposed to. There were no grades or praises from teachers, and I think that really scared me. I didn't know what pace I was supposed to move at or how I was supposed to know if what I was doing was right if there was no one there to tell me."

Feedback is vital to understanding the expectations of your team(s), being aware of current performance, and learning how to grow as a professional. As you move into new roles and develop skills in management, learning how to effectively give and receive feedback is a critical skill to have in the workplace.

Some companies have formalized review processes, others may have more casual reviews and feedback. In my experience, the more established the companies are, the more formalized the review processes. My time at a startup, however, had no review process. With no HR department or even a staff member focused on HR practices, there was little to no formalized anything. This complicated many dynamics.

Studies show millennials desire feedback and want to know where they stand. Growing up in a culture of instantaneous results, millennials expect to receive feedback more frequently. Interestingly, even though we desire more constant feedback, studies show we are less likely to ask for it.[2] We care about meaningful engagement at work, so it is beneficial to seek out the feedback that will help lead to better performance and stronger employee engagement.[3]

In college, professors handed out a syllabus, an assignment, and an expected due date. In the real world, we are responsible for seeking and clarifying information. In school, our grade let us know immediately how we performed. In the real world, we may not receive real-time feedback. Or any at all. It helps to build rapport with supervisors to discover an effective communication style.

For example, suppose you wanted feedback after a client presentation. You could wait to see if your boss says anything, but may never hear anything since people move on quickly to the next project or deliverable.

As a solution, you might ask in advance for real-time feedback. Or you could ask to sit down later in the week. This way, you help to set expectations with your manager and give them advance notice to pay attention so they can provide thoughtful notes. It all depends upon the communication and management style of your boss.

## WORK SCHEDULES AND CULTURES

Entering the working world radically changes our schedules. In college, we picked classes based on professors, time of day, or other factors. We joined organizations and arranged our schedule based on meetings. We worked in availability for sports or intramural team practices and games. We were in control of our own schedules. All that changes when we enter the working world.

For many new graduates, the idea that most of your life will consist of a forty-plus-hour work week Monday through Friday is daunting, if not downright depressing. As Dylan, a recent graduate, shared, "The scariest thing is the expansive nature of adulthood. It's like I can see ahead of me and it never ends."

Thankfully some elements about this new structure are freeing. Your weekends become actual weekends where you do not have to worry about homework, papers, or class projects. You may occasionally have to work additional hours or shifts, but overall, there is a more distinct separation of work hours and weekend hours.

Graduates find this to be a wonderful aspect of post-grad life. "Now that I know what it's like to have a full-time position and not have to worry about doing homework, the [evenings] are wonderful," said Chris. "I love relaxing and winding down and doing things I love to do."

"I had time to develop and cultivate hobbies I'd ignored in college and time to read for pleasure!" Rachel said. "It was incredible to feel like I actually owned my time."

The sense of ownership over time also relates to choosing our own vacation times versus having the weeks blocked out for us like they were in the educational system. Previously, vacation was set for you and breaks were frequent and long. Now, you are usually given a number of "paid time off" (PTO) days and must plan accordingly. No one will set vacation time for you or tell you that you should take it. You have to request time off and determine when, where, and how you take vacation. More about self-care later on, but please . . . take some vacation.

Fortunately, companies are increasingly implementing flexible policies and are working to instill various employee engagement initiatives to ensure their employees are successful holistically. Many companies accommodate their employees through unlimited PTO, work-from-home policies, and other company flexibility perks in order to retain staff and attract talent.

With technological advancements and access to communication tools outside of a physical office, working from home has naturally evolved as COVID-19 forced companies to adapt to government decrees that required all nonessential workers to work from home. Forced to reevaluate their policies, companies are becoming more open to a full-time or hybrid remote workforce.

Even prior to 2020, employees may have expected their employers to offer some type of work-from-home policy. The ability to work from home may shape an employee's decision to leave or join a company. Gallup research reveals that 51 percent of employees say they would switch to a job that allows them flextime.[4]

While remote work might be assumed as just a perk to improve company culture, it actually improves employee engagement, which ultimately drives performance. Working from home causes employees to feel more intentionally involved and can lead to an increase in productivity.[5] Employees who work from home tend to be happier and healthier, which ultimately leads to a decrease in employee turnover, saving companies money. Work-from-home or flexible working policies help employees feel as though their company considers their overall well-being, not just work output. As companies adapt to an influx of millennials and Gen Z in the workforce, employee engagement, flexibility, and company perks are becoming a priority amongst companies in order to attract and keep their talent.

Personally, prior to COVID-19, I really enjoyed working remotely. The flexibility helped me coordinate plans when I visited friends, traveled for a wedding, or spent time at home with family over the holidays. Knowing I could work from home for a day or two enabled me to find a more affordable flight and adapt my schedule based on the event.

As a result of COVID-19, I have stronger expectations to continue working remotely. I value the flexibility and freedom it provides while appreciating how it enables me to focus on the work without the distractions of an office environment.

Working from home also reduces the cost and time of commuting and allows fewer interruptions and distractions, not to mention the perk of throwing the occasional load of laundry into the machine while you work.

If your company permits remote work, make sure you understand the expectations of your supervisor(s) and effectively communicate about performance. "My current biggest challenge is adjusting to a job where I get to work from home!" said Kiernan. "I have lots of flexibility, which I love, and I want to make sure that I'm making the best use of my time always."

COVID-19 dramatically impacted the realities of remote work for employers. If they did not have policies already, companies likely created more standardized procedures for their employees to work from home, whether full time or allowing the option to choose.

Depending on your line of work, however, working remotely may not be a possibility for you. Even if COVID-19 changed things temporarily, perhaps your industry or profession is not conducive to work remotely full-time. You may be a surgeon or nurse and perform all your work at the hospital or clinic. You may be a teacher and need to be physically present in your classroom. You may be in graduate school and have to attend classes, practicums, and clinicals.

Working remotely is certainly a perk for some companies in providing flexibility. Another important component of a healthy workplace is developing quality relationships within the company, which ultimately helps to create a strong company culture.

We spend most of our time during the week working, and therefore communicating with our coworkers. It is no wonder the term *work family* is used to describe our work environment. Now more than ever, company culture is vitally important in attracting future and retaining current employees. With some companies, the culture includes strong employee engagement with programs, initiatives, and social events inside and outside of the workplace. Other companies may focus less on the culture and emphasize the work itself.

Job satisfaction is not limited to the subject matter and role itself. When you interview, it is important to learn what kind of environment you work best in because that will be where you spend much of your time and energy during the week.

Both of the agencies I worked for had an employee resource group who planned internal events, focused on culture, and discussed agency-wide initiatives. The larger companies provided mentors and fostered professional growth and opportunities to learn from one another. Internal gatherings allowed employees to engage with industry trends and discuss ways to promote and celebrate the work of teams and individuals.

Smaller companies may not have a structured HR department or cultural initiatives, but it will still be evident if the company values creating a positive and healthy environment for its employees.

Kent went to work at a young tech company after college and said: "My company isn't normal. They gave me a team three months in. They let me learn on the fly and fail forward. I love it." When asked what he did not expect about post-grad, he said, "How happy I would be at my job. Culture is king."

Unfortunately, not everyone has the same experience. "My work environment turned out to be crap," admitted Josiah. "I had six other associates in my building who I worked with each and every day. If you do not like the people you work within that tight knit of a group, you are in trouble."

What kind of work environment do you want? What kind of corporate culture do you thrive in? You may not know the answer until you experience different types of work environments.

Unless you work for yourself, you will have several relationships with coworkers and supervisors. As you change roles or jobs, you will continue to learn different working styles, forms of communication, and approaches to handling conflict. You will encounter and build relationships with many different people throughout your career. Remaining open minded and curious will help you learn more about yourself and others, which will benefit you in the workplace and beyond.

---

## CHAPTER 10

# IT'S A MARATHON, NOT A SPRINT

"The road goes ever on and on."

J. R. R. TOLKIEN

When we graduate college, we immediately put intense pressure on ourselves to find a job that aligns with our dreams and skills. Unfortunately, that first job is more often than not a wake-up call to reality. You may dislike your first job, or even hate it.

When asked what advice she would give to those who just graduated, Vanessa cautioned that first job will often be tolerable at best. "You're very likely going to feel like a failure for a large amount of this year. It's normal. Everyone I talked to has been feeling this way," she said. "It's really lonely and really scary and really hard."

Working in entry-level positions makes you feel disconnected from your goals and ambitions. With a focus on granular tasks, it may be difficult to see how your role ladders up to the company's strategy and mission. You may feel as though you are not living up to your potential, but keep in mind you are learning important skills and gaining valuable experiences that shape you as a young professional.

Dakota initially struggled adjusting to the never-ending routines of a full-time schedule. "Although I have gotten over the initial shock and disappointment of this job transition, it has been hard for me to keep a positive attitude about a job that does not challenge me, and in which I feel like I am not learning and growing, but rather handling simple admin tasks no one else has time for," Dakota said. "I understand the importance of these things, but I want to make an impact on people and the success of the business, so to be so far from it has been a hard pill to swallow."

There are a variety of factors that contribute to job likeability. No job is perfect, and no job will consist of everything you enjoy. However, there is a difference between navigating the challenges of a job and realizing the job is not a good fit. Jenny moved to Los Angeles without a job and felt the pressure to find something. "I took the first job I was offered and got stuck in that job for eight months where I was completely miserable and not in the field I wanted to be in."

Compared to an enjoyable college job or internship, the stark differences reveal how the job may simply not be a good fit. Wyatt confessed, "I hated my job in New York. It was even harder because I knew what it was like to love your job and to genuinely enjoy going to work every day since I had the amazing experience of spending the previous four years as a tour guide."

In those cases, remember a current job is not the same as your entire career. It may feel like it in the present, but look beyond your current circumstances to gain perspective. Your entire career is not defined by that one job. Entry-level positions often provide a springboard into another role or company, and you can always use it to pivot in a different direction. Do not be afraid to take action to change your situation.

Rachel landed the job she thought she wanted, but once in it, she questioned whether or not she wanted to pursue a career in the industry. "The actual, real-life, full-time job didn't satisfy me in the way I thought it would," she said. "I soon found myself struggling to envision a future in which I was still writing about television thirty years down the road. Or even five years down the road. Or even . . . one year down the road." Rachel decided to leave her job and focus her career in a different field. While she never expected to change her path so quickly, she was glad she had the courage to change her direction proactively.

Staying at or leaving a company is often driven by work environments. Both millennials and Gen Z desire for their jobs to consist of professional growth and a healthy company culture. Employee engagement and internal communications strategies are becoming more prioritized in the workplace. Companies are committing entire departments and roles for people to focus on these initiatives.

According to Gallup, 87 percent of millennials say professional development and career-growth opportunities are important to a job.[2] More than previous generations, finding a job with development opportunities is vital in both attracting and retaining the employee. Young professionals want their workplaces to be a place where they can learn and develop.

As an art director in advertising, Beth changed jobs because she felt like she was not growing at her previous company. "My career path wasn't clear, I wasn't receiving the mentorship I sought, and after three-plus years, I was ready for a change," Beth said. "I'm at a bigger company now with many more people and many more resources. It was important to me to have the experience of a small company and now a global one, and ultimately decide which environment I feel more comfortable in, now and later in life."

While younger generations in the workforce can be criticized for changing jobs frequently, the reality is that we desire to feel connected to our company, colleagues, and work. We would like to advance in our career. We want to grow.

"The main challenges I have had in my career is lack of development and investment," said Nick. "For three years I had to figure out how to do my job with little guidance or help. The help I did get, I would never know if it was actually helping or not because I never had a performance review, and business was slow in the industry anyway."

It is quite common to feel disengaged due to a lack of investment in employee growth and development, especially from a manager or the company's leadership. In fact, one out of every two employees has left a job to get away from a manager, according to Gallup's State of the American Manager report.[3]

Teachers play a vital role in a student's education, so naturally, managers are no different for the impact they have in our careers. Unfortunately, far too often some of the most challenging aspects within a workplace are tied to the supervisory relationship.

"I've had some pretty terrible jobs right out of college—and none of them were about the jobs themselves. They were all about my coworkers, my managers, or the company culture. I had enough of feeling like it was all out of my control, and that is why I decided to move to freelancing," said Emily. She used the connections she made while at the company and began to work for herself.

Lori spoke of how that relational investment from a manager can pay off—if you are fortunate enough to have it. "I've realized the biggest thing I value in a job is a fantastic supervisor. My current boss always has my back, listens to my ideas, and works to make sure I feel valued and fulfilled. I had no idea how big a deal this would be, but having someone so supportive as a mentor and boss can make a tough job so much more rewarding. She energizes me, and I want to do well in my job for her," she explained.

"When starting out in your career," said Campbell, "I think it's really important to have a boss or mentor who is looking out for you and who you can look up to. I attribute much of my career success to others who have shown me the way, and I've been able to adapt, grow, and emulate the way they conduct their roles."

If you do not have the best relationship with your boss or direct supervisor but do not have the opportunity to change jobs, try to build relationships with other colleagues at the office. You can find mentors who support you and want the best for you, even if you do not work directly with them. Mentorship may happen outside of your specific department, company, or industry. It can be eye opening to learn from others who have gone before you.

Beyond specific relationships, the entire workplace environment can sometimes be toxic. When the work culture and relationships are unhealthy, it trickles into your life outside of your professional one. Brett decided to leave a negative work environment. "Toxic workplaces burned me out and bled into my personal life and even future jobs," he said. "It made me paranoid and short fused."

It is not easy to leave a job due to an unhealthy environment. Charlie was working as a medical scribe at a hospital to obtain patient care hours for Physician Assistant school, which she enjoyed. But the people and atmosphere left her feeling overly stressed and worried. "Even though this job looked so appealing for PA school, I finally knew I had to part ways," Charlie shared. "I put my two weeks' notice in this month, and I have honestly never felt so relieved. I knew I did the right thing for myself."

It may take first-hand experience to know how to avoid those environments in the future. When you interview for future jobs, you can ask questions about the work culture to discern whether or not it is a healthy workplace. You can learn to listen to *how* someone describes their job functions, team culture, and overall work environment. For instance, if you are leaving your current position because of capacity issues, be sure to ask about work-life balance, typical hours, flexibility, and workload for the future position. If you are leaving because of a lack of growth opportunities, ask about professional development, mentorship, or paths for career growth. If you are leaving because of poor management, ask both the hiring manager and those on the team about the culture, communication styles, and expectations within the team environment.

Ben was overworked by his previous employer because his team was under resourced. When interviewing, he knew how to ask questions to get a sense of the work-life balance. "Asking the right questions if you're leaving for specific reasons is key in those interviews," said Ben. "You don't want to walk into the same situation somewhere else."

You have the power to ask bold and direct questions in interviews. Questions can be simple, such as "What do you enjoy most about your job?" or "What has been challenging or something you wish you could change?" or "What has been the most fulfilling aspect of your job so far?" Often, these reflective questions will provide you with a glimpse into the team's authentic answers. Those kinds of questions can tell you a lot of what you need to know.

## NOT ACCORDING TO PLAN

When we enter the world of work, we cannot anticipate the specific circumstances and challenges we will face.

One challenge can be dealing with the consequences of exiting teammates often leaving behind a trail of responsibilities to be redistributed. "I started off very happy, just eager to learn and grow," Gina said. "Suddenly, my coworker left the company, and I was chosen to take on all her tasks, and I became swamped with everything. It was very hard for me to keep organized and meet deadlines. I wasn't happy with the work I was doing, my voice wasn't heard when I came up with ideas and creative thoughts, I felt like I wasn't doing meaningful work, I felt like I was being underpaid for all the work I took on, I didn't have a good relationship with my manager or my CMO."

Sometimes unforeseen circumstances interfere with career plans. Caroline was recruited by the FBI and accepted the job, but ran into one bureaucratic obstacle after another. "The trouble was it required security clearance, and they had never hired graduates straight out of college before. I ended up in the middle of a complete and total disaster. I was originally supposed to start a job in San Francisco in July after graduation. Know when I finally got my official offer? . . . Sixteen months after the original offer. In that time, my social security number was stolen by China (thank you, OPM), they lost my fingerprints (so those are floating around somewhere), they lost my email, and they totally failed to communicate with me. I was left post-grad with a 'job' and no actual job. I ended up working part time at a yoga studio, volunteering at a library, and actively avoiding anyone who might ask me what was happening in my life because I just got so tired of explaining that I kind of had a job but not really, and that it could happen any day (which is what they told me for fourteen months)." Caroline explained, "I felt inadequate, embarrassed, lost, and sad."

Nothing can ever prepare you to deal with such a rollercoaster.

One of the hardest aspects of adjusting to the real world—and one of the most challenging aspects of life—is that we cannot control what happens after we choose a job. You cannot predict downsizing and being laid off from your job. You cannot predict changes to your role, your team, or your management. You cannot predict economic events that affect the job marketplace or your industry. You certainly could never have predicted a global pandemic where more than fifty million people would file for first-time unemployment benefits.[4]

"I struggled so much in the waiting for what was next: waiting for applications to open, waiting to hear back from schools (rejection), ending up on the waitlist at one school close to home and not making it through, waiting for the next cycle of applications to open up, waiting to hear back again, etc.," said Mackenzie, a grad student. "All the while I was working an in-between job that was not fulfilling and was only a means to an end. A lot of the time I felt as though

I wasn't living for my 'now' but for the future me. Everything was about a future I wasn't even sure would happen."

We can make plans, but they will change. These are the moments in which our strength, character, and resiliency will be tested. How we adapt and persevere will shape our future, perhaps more than the disappointment itself.

## DELAYED CAREER GROWTH

The speed of job growth is often not at all what you anticipate. You will not receive a promotion each year like you did in school as you moved into a new grade. Negotiations during the offer process can be overwhelming, especially early in your careers. After you accept an offer and the base salary is set, it becomes more difficult to grow from that number.

When you accepted the job, you might have been so ecstatic to have an offer that you did not want to push your luck by negotiating the offered salary. Or maybe you were afraid of the negotiation process and how asking for more money would impact someone's perception of you. Or maybe you even had multiple offers and were able to evaluate components from competing job offers, which can be advantageous for negotiation.

"I think it's particularly important to learn how to advocate for yourself and fight for what you're worth," said Allison. "One of the best pieces of advice I ever received was to never accept a job without negotiating!"

Once you begin a new job, keep track of your key contributions or accomplishments. If you work in a fast-paced environment, set aside time to record those insights and data every quarter. Most reviews, where salary is most frequently discussed, typically occur annually. No one will be more aware of your contributions than you.

Typically, companies have a standardized process for reviews. HR or your supervisor may reach out to colleagues who work with you to gain feedback. Taking time to complete your own self-evaluation will prepare you to know the value you bring to the company. If your company does peer interviews, you may need to clarify or provide more context about a point made by a colleague. Documentation also helps if you need to dispute something said during the feedback process. Your personal record of accomplishments tracked throughout the year can be used to support why a title change or salary increase is justified.

Learning to negotiate your salary is a key growth experience in the workforce, regardless of whether your company has a step plan for years of experience or merit increases. It is vital to advocate for yourself, especially when it comes to appropriate compensation and overall value as an employee. It is no one else's job to advocate for you, and even if you have a great manager, you need to learn how to be your own advocate.

June learned how to have productive conversations with her manager about how her worth as an employee translates into pay. "I think I've felt like asking for more money is greedy, and unappreciative of what I have, but in reality, that's part of life and part of a job," she said. "As cliché as it is, the answer will always be no unless you ask."

During her review, Annie was encouraged to counter her promotion offer after being coached through the process by a friend. "It served me well at the moment, as my company exceeded my counter, and I've noticed a pivotal change in the way I am viewed at work by my boss and their bosses," she said. "I am able to step more into my potential at work, while feeling proud of the process to get there too."

A common challenge faced by young professionals is lack of promotion or career development. "When I've intentionally changed jobs, I did a lot of weighing what my opportunity was for growth in each opportunity," Allison said. "Ultimately, I moved on because the next step was a chance to grow and was a better fit for my strengths and passions."

Your growth is important too. There can be a sense of duty to a company, especially when you have benefitted from working there. "Stockholm syndrome sets in a little bit when you've been with a company for a long time and you start to feel the need to 'owe' them something—your allegiance, your work ethic, your time," observed Kristi. "News flash I've more recently learned, you don't! You are the only one looking out for y-o-u in your career path."

More often than not, a company cares more about their own interests than your own growth. After all, it is a business. As Elijah said, "A company is a collection of parts (people). Your 'job' is to play a role in that collection, so stay mindful of the fact that your best interest as an individual can never be the top priority of a company."

While the employer may provide resources, growth opportunities, and time for professional development, the goal of most businesses is to focus on their own profitability, market share, product lines, or services development. They may foster a healthy culture, but as an afterthought.

"You may think your company, boss or coworkers care about you, but you still need to be your own biggest advocate and fight for what you deserve," said Avery. "If a company can use you without compensating you accordingly, they will."

"It was way harder than I had planned," Charlie said after his first few years out of college, "especially after my family-friendly firm merged and I was treated as another fish in the sea being overworked and underappreciated making them money and giving myself anxiety and stress."

Yes, you need humility and a willingness to learn, but you also need to understand your value and what you can offer a company and team.

Advocating for yourself is even more important when you are self-employed or have your own company. As a freelance videographer in Los Angeles, Zachary had to understand his value so he could price his work accordingly as he booked clients. "I didn't think after graduating that I was worth anything yet, thought I was back at square one, a freshman in life," Zachary said. "You've got to own all that you have to offer, then people will see that in you."

Knowing your value takes time and practice to develop as a professional skill. Sometimes, that comes through learning to say no. "The biggest lesson I've learned," said Cassie, "is probably how to say no for myself—to take ownership of what I want and what I need and be able to clearly communicate that. Standing up for yourself and having respect for yourself and believing in yourself are hard to master. Literally everything is a lesson."

Bottom line: your employer or client pays you to provide a service. When you peel back all the layers, it is as simple as that. You feel a sense of pride and accomplishment when the service you provide is valued. If you are not appropriately compensated or valued for that service, it will lead to frustration and disengagement.

"I think most companies will always try to get away with giving you the bare minimum to keep you happy (kudos to the companies that don't do this)," Peyton said. "I think I've learned you always need to be asking for more and challenging your employer to let them know you won't be happy with the bare minimum."

While your worth is not measured by a salary or job title, it can lead to inner confidence and a healthy sense of accomplishment. "There will always be a battle between money, job fulfillment, and respect." Beatriz said. "Money doesn't buy happiness, but it does make things a lot easier. But also feeling valued and respected at a job, even though it may not be 100 percent fulfilling, goes a long way."

A job is more than salary and benefits. Whether it is work-life balance, company culture, or growth opportunities, pay attention to what you value. If those values don't line up with your job, the incongruence is disappointing. Instead of complaining and not attempting change, we need to learn how to speak up in the workplace.

Before getting married, Hadley was unsure whether she could continue working at her company because her soon-to-be husband was finishing medical school in a different city. She explained the situation to her boss and was allowed to work remotely for a few months so she could be in the same city as her new husband. After a few months, they both moved to Chicago and continued their transition into marriage in the same city. As Hadley commented, "Things can get better if you speak up for yourself. Being bold for what you want/need to make you happy in a job is important."

It was evident that the company valued her and was willing to adjust to make it possible. But she had to have the courage to ask.

## WHEN YOU LEAVE YOUR JOB

How do you know when it is an ideal time to change jobs? Even if you feel ready for a change, the thought of another job search is overwhelming. After all, most people are all too familiar with how brutal the process can be.

Thankfully, you have more experience under your belt, more connections on LinkedIn, and a better sense of the type of role and environment you want compared to when you were twenty-two years old.

Especially for the millennial and Gen Z generations, it is very common to change jobs, or even industries, multiple times throughout your career. According to the Bureau of Labor Statistics, the median tenure of workers ages twenty-five to thirty-four is 2.8 years.[5] Stories from my survey respondents confirmed this pattern.

"I am on my fifth job in eight years. Yup, you read that right. For all but one of those changes, I was in the driver seat. I was able to leave for a better opportunity. And that opportunity typically meant more money," said Peter. "But as time has gone on, I have taken a much more long-term approach to finding a new role. There is so much more that goes into my decision-making than just money. It's a mixture of both the tangibles (think money and benefits), as well as the intangibles (work/life balance, possibility for advancement, learning opportunities, overall development of my career outside of just earning potential)."

Changing jobs several times in a short span of time can bring a sense of shame. I know I felt it. While several changes were a result of circumstances beyond my control, I did end up switching jobs much more than I ever anticipated or wanted. Including my time at the coffee shop, I worked a total of five jobs in the first six years after graduation. Not exactly the path I pictured for myself when I first dreamed about my career.

"Since graduating college eight years ago, I've had four jobs," said Mary. "I've definitely struggled with having so many jobs, maybe because our parents' generation took a job and stuck with it for better or for worse, and I feel like I've been always jumping around when I'm looking for more of a challenge. A lot of the jobs I have been in haven't had many areas for growth within the company. Through each job change, I've learned what is important to me in a job—work-life balance, coworkers, and environment."

These new jobs help identify attributes most important to you.

"It was helpful to have experience under my belt when interviewing for my new job because I now had an idea of what I liked/disliked in the workplace," said Brittany. "I was able to speak more confidently about my goals and expectations."

Ideally, as we develop a strong network of colleagues over time, we can reach out to other professionals who may know of opportunities or who can refer you internally to their HR departments. When the role is in the same city, referrals can be particularly beneficial, but people can still act as a contact even if they are in a different state.

Compared to the job search after college, your network now is broader and more personal, which acts as a stronger resource in this job search.

Another benefit in this time of job searching is that more pieces of our lives are now established. Immediately after college, almost all aspects of life were up in the air. As you progress throughout your twenties and thirties, there are fewer question marks about your life needing to be solved at one time.

Despite these benefits, it may surprise you that the job search still takes time. If you are recruited by a company, that might make the process smoother, although the application process can still take several weeks or months. There are often multiple rounds of interviews and a test, case study, or project to highlight your expertise. The process requires patience and mental perseverance.

"Finally reaching that decision to start looking is also a really difficult process. It's an uneasy journey toward your tipping point because you don't really know what it is until you reach that point," said Dominique. "And the time commitment to find a job is really tough—updating your résumé, completing applications, networking, talking with your mentors, looking for jobs that look okay, doing interviews and coffee dates, etc."

Perspective is key. "Early on in your career, be quick to make a change if your job is not what you want or not challenging you," advised Grayson. "It's easy to get comfortable, but if you aren't [consciously] building your résumé, the job you really want will be even more difficult to get. It's also incredibly difficult not to look to your left or your right and compare yourself against how others are doing. A career is a marathon and where you are at twenty-five will be very different than fifty."

To combat the fears of changing jobs, Shane recommended you gain all the experiences you can in your first ten years of your career. "After that, we get too expensive on the payroll to start over, and it's much more difficult to significantly switch gears," he said. "If you get different experiences early, even if it's a negative experience, it's much easier to leverage when we're at higher levels later in our careers."

When you do decide to change jobs, it comes with complex emotions—excitement for the new opportunity, yet sadness over what you're leaving behind—coworkers who became friends, a boss who became a professional mentor, and years of experience where you built a career. Understandably, you can feel a sense of loss; changing jobs is a major life change.

"Changing jobs is one of the hardest things to do," Brianna acknowledged. "Especially when you love the work that you are creating and there are peers who have become family. It becomes something you know you have to do in order to progress forward, versus something that you necessarily want to do. It's always bittersweet."

Changing jobs means a change in your comfort zone. Many young professionals felt their work provided a sense of home. "In my experience, it was scary to leave a 'home' I had created over four years. Not just relationships, but knowing what to do and the ins and outs of the company made me super comfortable," Mike said. "Overcoming comfort was the hardest part of job searching."

"My first job truly felt like 'home' to me," Jake said. "I loved the people. I loved the work. But I didn't love the idea about staying in the city I was in. I began looking elsewhere and eventually made the move. Quitting my first job felt like a breakup, truly."

It can be extremely terrifying to quit your job. We may feel ready for the change, but we often underestimate how comfortable and familiar our rhythms had become with that role. It is difficult to leave the familiar for the uncertain.

"I found a new job that would allow me to pursue my long-term goals and bring us to a city where we may find more like-minded people," said Emmanuel. Still, he added, "Quitting your first job is terrifying—like kicking the ground out from under you!"

It might be tough to take the plunge and switch jobs, but the rewards are worth it. After feeling discontented, Gavin proceeded to make a change in his career and could not be happier with the decision. "I have a great supporting cast of coworkers, a job that allows me to learn more each day, and a career that has a good, upward trajectory," he said. "I am happy to go in each day and appreciate that I made the change."

Jake was glad he took his first job. Even though not a dream job, it was a place to start and to learn. "I think I realized that everything and every opportunity is a stepping stone, and none of it is wasted. If I were to somehow 'wait around' for my absolute dream job right out of college . . . I don't know that I would have ended up where I am today," he said. "Starting somewhere is still starting. And had I not started where I did, although it wasn't a 'dream,' I may not have made it 'to' my dream later on."

Our fears can keep us from taking action or risks, especially in making proactive changes in our lives. It's scary to make the decision to change jobs or careers, especially when you do not know the outcome. But if we let go of the pressure or expectation to have it all figured out, we can remember each job is a learning experience that helps us grow and move toward our desired direction. Do not be discouraged. Change takes time—and a change could be exactly what you need.

In ideal circumstances, you have a sense of control over the timing and way you choose the next job. But sometimes, the unexpected happens.

## WHEN YOUR JOB LEAVES YOU

Accepting a job offer provides such a good feeling—a sense of accomplishment, of relief, and of excitement over the future. Once starting a new job, the possibility of being laid off or fired rarely crosses your mind. But layoffs happen, especially in an unstable economy. Financial security or stability can be threatened as companies merge, downsize, or acquire another company. Market shifts or changes in staff can also lead to adjustments in jobs, open positions, or departments. Between recessions and stock-market crashes, the instability of the job market often leads to instability in our own personal lives.

Some industries are affected in times of economic uncertainty more than others, but a new wave of unemployment shocked the nation due to the impacts of COVID-19. The economic effects of city lockdowns and social-distancing precautions greatly impacted a variety of markets in unprecedented ways. Layoffs skyrocketed, with over fifty-four million people (approximately 33 percent of the workforce) filing initial jobless claims by the end of July 2020.[6] In a matter of months, those fifty-four million unemployed claims far surpassed the thirty-seven million filed during the eighteen-month Great Recession.[7]

After a layoff due to the pandemic, Kristi shared her initial reactions. "I only have four days of laid-off experience to speak about, but it's been humbling, to say the least," she said. "The shame and embarrassment, even, I've felt over something that's supposed to be incredibly impersonal has been eye opening."

Most pandemic-related job losses were due to extraordinary outside forces rather than any individual performance issues. Never before have entire industries been so gravely impacted. But just because millions of people were affected does not make a layoff any easier.

How we respond to a loss often reveals what we value. As a society, we highly value our careers. According to a Zapier study, most Gen Zers (65 percent) and millennials (73 percent) said their job is a major component of their personal identity.[8] Whether we realize it or not, our identity and worth are intertwined with our job titles, salaries, and overall status within a company.

"Our culture puts way too much stock in career achievement and identity. Also, we expect if we work hard to be rewarded for the investment. It doesn't always work that way," observed Chase. "Nurses and teachers are some of the most important jobs, and they're not compensated well."

We let a description of our position give us more value than a description of our character. Bianca recalled being asked at the doctor's office if she worked full or part time. "I stammered through answering 'not employed—but I'm in between roles!' as if I needed to prove myself to the scheduling nurse?" she said.

There is a deep-rooted connection between our jobs and our identity, and that sense of worth gets rattled if the status abruptly moves to "unemployed." Who are we if we cannot respond to a question about what we do for a living?

"You are not your job. I struggled with this after being laid off from my first job after finishing grad school and moving to Chicago," admitted Dominic. "I had to come to the realization that I was always going to be a designer regardless of if I were working full time for a company or not. Not only that, I'm more than a designer."

Your job is a part of you, but there is so much more to you than your employment status, job title, or paycheck. You are a complex human being with a variety of interests, skills, and passions. Your identity is not limited to your profession.

"Your job will never be as important as you are—or your relationships," Abby said. "Give your career your best but don't give it your all—as in, don't sacrifice what really makes life worth living."

After being suddenly laid off, I can confidently say that jobs and money will come and go—we cannot base our worth and value off of our job titles, company names, and salaries. While those accomplishments are worth celebrating, they cannot be our identity. Because suddenly, one day, all of that can change and you're left without those same titles, company names, and salaries you once valued.

Even if you know logically a layoff can happen, nothing can prepare you for the loss and shock when a job is suddenly gone. Amelia moved to New York City after college and lost her job unexpectedly. "Here I was, in one of the most expensive cities in the world, without any income," she said. "I wish I knew how tough it actually was to get a job. Even living and having previous work experience in NYC, it still took me three months after being laid off to find a new job. It's ruthless!"

Naseem worked in Silicon Valley and lost both jobs she had after college. After six months at a recruiting firm, everyone was suddenly laid off. She ended up a disheartening few months later at a tech startup in San Francisco. "I was employee number ten and we expanded to fifty-five! I moved to San Francisco and lived there for 2.5 years. It was the best time of my life. After three-ish years, our company was again dissolved suddenly. I had to move home because I couldn't afford rent in San Francisco, lost a ton of friendships, and was just stuck again in this pattern of getting laid off." Naseem said. "Definitely takes a toll on your ego and worth."

Julia worked at an exciting, growing company in New York that changed in a day when she was laid off unexpectedly. "The biggest surprise for me," she said, "was the hit my ego took—and I will always remember who reached out and who didn't in the days after."

Sudden job loss is a shocking, traumatic event. There are multiple stages of grief, but there is no expected timeline or typical path to move through those stages. Grief is not linear.

On the day that I was laid off, I called my parents outside the office building and then went for a walk nearby. As I walked along Lake Michigan and eventually the Riverwalk, I called a few friends from college to share the news with them. As I described what happened, I did so without emotion or awareness of how much my life would change. Friends who saw me on the first day were surprised to see me "handling it so well." I was even asked by a friend if I was faking it, which made me realize how I was in a genuine state of denial.

As the initial shock began to wear off, I moved into the next stages of grief. I felt overwhelmed after I suspended my student loans and filed for unemployment benefits. I was angry and wondered if I had done anything to cause this to happen to me. Or anything I could have done differently to avoid this. I wrestled with emotions of worthlessness and thoughts of being a failure.

As the months went on and the disappointments in my career continued, I felt stuck in a cycle with the situation only getting worse. While I wanted to believe another opportunity would come along, I could not see how that was possible at the time. Sometimes, my perspective was clouded; all I could see was the loss.

A layoff removes the context of relationships with coworkers and clients. You leave behind months or years at that workplace, often without any warning. You are rarely given any closure when forced to leave that day, or even that hour. You leave behind visions for your future and plans for your career. You lose a source of income in an instant. You no longer have your routine, comfort, and sense of normalcy. All of it, lost.

A layoff can feel like your entire life was shattered into pieces, and you are left on your own to put them back together. Let yourself grieve. Take it one day at a time. And do not let this define you. A layoff may be one part of your story, but it is never the whole story.

I've learned to accept a layoff at twenty-three years old as a part of my story. While I often wish it never happened in the first place, I've seen how it has been a source of connection within my community. Friends have introduced me to others who have struggled with job loss, unemployment, and career uncertainty. I continue to find meaning and purpose in my career journey as I share my story with others. I bet this book would not exist otherwise.

## CHAPTER 11

# LIFE IS NOT
# A ROM-COM

"We are biologically, cognitively,
physically, and spiritually wired
to love, to be loved and to belong."

BRENÉ BROWN

Our work may answer the question about *what* we do with our lives, but our relationships answer the question with *whom* we spend our lives.

As we navigate our relationships in adulthood, we experience a variety of challenges, obstacles, and growth opportunities—not unlike the lessons we learn in our careers. When we decided on a career path, we chose to work in a specific field or industry. We spent time, energy, and effort in pursuit of that direction.

Even though most decisions in life are not completely irreversible, your choices matter. A decision about one job leads to specific work experiences and contacts, which direct your next job and ultimately shape the trajectory of your career.

Similarly, the transition into our adulthood provides a new way of building and investing in community, which particularly impacts our friendships and relationships. Throughout our twenties and thirties, we make key relationship decisions that establish and direct our future, especially as it relates to a long-term partner.

Relationships equip us to learn about healthy expectations, communication styles, and conflict-resolution tactics with another human being. One relationship could be a learning opportunity for the next, or it could lead to a life-long commitment.

As we date in our twenties, we discover what attributes we desire in a life partner. Even if we do not get married in your twenties—even if we do not get married at all—we are learning valuable lessons through our relationships, romantic or otherwise.

Our career pathways diverge in various directions; it is the same for relationships within the various life stages of singleness, dating, and marriage. And these changes occur mostly within our twenties and early thirties. According to the US Census Bureau, the average age for marriage recently reached its highest point on record: thirty years for men and twenty-eight for women.[2]

Several reasons contribute to this delay in marriage, such as the number of young adults, especially women, gaining a college education and the emphasis on building a career before settling down. Additionally, the reality of the economy, the increase of cohabitation, and the desire to develop financial stability affect timing for when adults choose to get married.

While there is a delay compared to previous generations, most of these life changes are still experienced in the first decade following college graduation. Based upon recent census data, 60 percent of women and 73 percent of men identify as never having been married at twenty-five years old. Five years later, the number decreased to 37 percent of women and 47 percent of men aged thirty to thirty-four who had never been married. By age thirty-five, the number dwindled to 23.5 percent of women and 28.9 percent of men.[3]

Fact is, the majority of adults will marry within the first decade after college. These years of our lives will consist of a highly concentrated time of navigating relationship changes as people date, break up, and eventually get married. Romantic relationships are a major part of what we experience in the transition into adulthood.

Despite the recent delays in marriage, school environments still prove to be a viable way to meet a partner. A Facebook Data Sciences study revealed about 28 percent of married graduates attended the same college as their spouse, and 15 percent of individuals attended the same high school.[4] While the average age to get married is increasing, a large number of young adults still marry someone they met in high school or college.

College is the last time we are surrounded by thousands of like-minded peers in such a compact area. Talk about some quality dating material.

You may have felt pressure to find someone during college because you heard how difficult it is to meet someone afterward. These societal pressures fluctuate based upon the region, such as Elizabeth's experience growing up in Texas. "I was afraid of not ever meeting a husband, because more often than not, we are bombarded with messages of 'finding your college sweetheart' and sweet, romantic stories of 'oh, we had a class together and it was fate!'" she said. "College seemed like the easiest, most probable place, even statistic-wise, where there would be a concentrated area of single young men."

And yet, many of us do not find our happily-ever-after in college. Graduating as a single woman gave me the confidence and freedom to move to Chicago without worrying how that decision would impact someone else. I easily began a new chapter of my life because I did not have to factor someone else into that decision.

The tension of maintaining a relationship and building a career remains throughout your twenties, but it is first felt in this initial transition. College can be a meaningful time to learn about yourself and a relationship, but you will eventually have to decide whether or not you will stay together after graduation. Uncertainty in a relationship and whether it could go the distance often complicates the post-graduation decisions. In order to stay together, seniors have to incorporate someone else's plans into their own. Some people try to find jobs in the same cities to live together and others realize their respective jobs will result in a long-distance relationship.

Aubrey and Matt, who met in college, confronted the uncertainties of what would happen to their relationship after their senior year. Aubrey said at the time, "I am also faced with a lot of unknowns because I do not know where my boyfriend of 2.5 years is moving to yet." She said, "I feel prepared to be independent, but am uncertain about my relationship. I want to make it work no matter where he ends up, but I know that at some point we will have to make compromises for us both to end up in the same city."

While there were many challenges, they continued their relationship after college and celebrated their marriage years later. Your twenties can be an ideal time for a long-distance relationship because you are able to establish yourself in your new job and city while still having the emotional support of someone else. The distance can be worth the effort.

Other graduating seniors come to the difficult decision to break up when their career pathways pulled them apart. As Zoey recalled, "I had to let go of a very meaningful romantic relationship because as in love as we were, life was taking us in two different directions. Knowing that we were only twenty-three and knowing that we weren't ready to give up on global opportunities for a relationship was heartbreaking."

The tension, however, exists throughout our twenties as we navigate relationships in the midst of ongoing changes and transitions. We develop more into our careers, foster a sense of community, and come into our own as adults. Once you are in the real world, dating becomes even more intentional as it naturally leads to the next stage of life: finding a partner.

## KEY RELATIONSHIP DECISIONS

The twenties are a peculiar time of life. Some friends are committing to spend the rest of their lives with someone. Other friends are not the least bit interested in a serious relationship.

Casey started dating someone after graduating college and discovered the differences in their intentionality. She said, "After three months of dating he started talking about getting married within the year and starting a family. I broke up with him shortly after." Casey did not want to settle down and raise a family at that time.

Conversely, Rebecca did want to marry and settle down after college but realized how much uncertainty still existed in her life. "I'm married now, which many people believe is 'arriving' at adulthood and maturity," she said. "But I'm still trying to figure out how to help support our family and find what I'm gifted at."

Marriage does not end the uncertainty in your life.

Singleness is a valuable time to learn more about yourself, to focus on your career, and to develop new skills and hobbies. You can grow in self-awareness and build confidence in your strengths and your weaknesses. With more flexibility and time, you can purposefully invest in the community around you. Singleness can be an empowering time. When you are single, you have the advantage to focus on becoming the right person instead of just waiting for the right person.

Most of the time, I wholeheartedly love my singleness. I love investing in my friendships. I love being spontaneous. I love having flexibility and availability in my schedule. I recognize that I have a capacity to do things many of my dating and married friends do not have, and for that I am grateful for the benefits of singleness.

When most around you are also single, you are not confronted with the relational changes as much. During the first few years after college, I attended a lot of larger group hangouts, events, and dinners. We traveled together and easily took hiking or camping trips. I remember those times fondly, knowing we were all in a similar life stage and could spontaneously gather together.

As people enter their late twenties, there is a subtle shift. "I think most twenty-somethings experience the liberation of *not* being married at twenty-five, and then at twenty-six being like wait . . . I don't even have a boyfriend!" Savannah said. "Then often we start to seriously date, hoping to meet a great guy and realizing that's super difficult, and then in our late twenties starting to have that moment of whoa . . . am I ever going to get married?"

As friends marry, the number of single friends quickly starts to dwindle. Like a domino effect, it can feel isolating if you are not even dating anyone. When engagement announcements are posted on social media or another "Save the date" arrives in the mail, it is a reminder of the stark differences in life stages. Finding a life partner is far from a reality in your own life.

Attending weddings at twenty-four or twenty-five years old was a blast with a big crowd of young people dancing for hours on end. As I've grown older, attending weddings has begun to feel different. I may be the only single person at a table of couples during the reception. Instead of a big group dancing, there are couples paired off with each other. Once a slow dance song comes on, the couples step forward. I step back and sit down. While I still absolutely love attending weddings, those are small moments where I began to notice I am single and a lot of my friends are not.

The reality of my singleness was most revealed to me when I attended sixteen weddings in one year. Yes, you read that right. Sixteen. Showing up for my friends on their wedding day was rewarding and fulfilling, and I would do it again in a heartbeat, but I would be lying to say it was not also exhausting, both physically and emotionally.

Within the span of that one year, marriage and romantic love were ever present in front of me. Celebrating friends getting married, alongside many friends who were dating or already married, naturally provoked thoughts about my own relationship status. As content as I have been in my singleness, I had to face my own emotions and desires. It forced me to admit that I wanted a relationship for myself.

Abra said, "I did see a lot of people getting married, so that led to some melodramatic conversations with friends about singledom and finding the one and marriage and settling down, but that I think will come and go over the next few years depending on where I am and what my relationship status is."

Alissa has been single for a few years. "There are periods where I desire a relationship and periods where I'm very content and happy with my singleness," said Alissa. "It's completely okay to be in either stage, and it will likely ebb and flow."

In the midst of changing circumstances, be honest with yourself about what you desire and be aware of your own emotions. Georgia moved to San Francisco after college, and for the first several years she did not think about dating much at all. She was focused on adjusting to new rhythms in a new job, environment, and time zone. "In the past year-ish, though, I've felt some feelings of wanting to be in a relationship soon," she said. "I've learned that instead of pushing my thoughts/feelings away, it is important to be curious about them!"

Sometimes we do not want to admit this desire because we do not want to seem desperate or because we want to hold on to our independence. Wanting a partner and hoping for companionship are normal desires.

The message to "Be content in your singleness" is conflicting when no one tells married couples to "Be content in your marriage." I hope to be content in all my circumstances, whether I am single or married. Contentment does not eliminate desire.

Humans are complex beings. Our multitude of emotions can coexist, even if they initially feel contradicting. We can learn to appreciate the value of our current circumstances while still hoping and desiring for them to change.

Extended seasons of singleness—especially perpetual singleness—can be disheartening. It is tempting to push away desires when you do not see them come to fruition. When singleness is your norm, it is common to numb yourself to the constant pain of disappointment. It becomes difficult to hope for a change in circumstance. This delay can be especially challenging as you approach, and pass, the age of thirty, a common benchmark many have in mind for reaching certain milestones.

As dating shifts to more intentionality, marriage becomes the end goal. Having a timeline only increases the source of internal pressures. Ian reflected back on the pressures he felt and how he viewed dating with a scarcity mentality. "In my head, I had to be married before thirty, otherwise all the 'good' ones would be taken," he said. "Of course, that was all false, and many of the relationships I saw broke up, and now I'm one of the youngest people in my current group to be married. I put undue pressure on myself to 'catch up,' which was false."

Pressure with timing and societal expectations especially hits women because it relates to having children by a certain age. Mary said, "I definitely feel a sense of a ticking clock, maybe more so just because of the baby factor, and biologically I only have so much time."

Similarly, Kylie discussed how it has been difficult to watch friends marry and have children, wondering if she should be on the same page as them. "We start to have this expectation of when we 'should' be married and having kids," she said. "However, life doesn't work that way since relationships are very unpredictable at times."

No wonder singleness can become increasingly difficult as we age. Choosing a partner, however, is one of the most important decisions we will make as adults. We are intentionally selecting who will be the most significant relationship in our lives, and that decision should not be rushed or made due to societal pressure.

On the other hand, instead of passively waiting, we can take initiative with our dating lives. It is brave to want something and to pursue it. When you want a career change, you network, spend time on applications, and actively make the switch. If you want a change in your relationship status, it also requires intentionality and effort.

## ACTIVELY PARTICIPATING IN ROMANCE

When the time feels right to pursue or be open to dating, many individuals turn to dating apps. The once-negative stigma of online dating has quickly shifted into the expected norm for millennials and Gen Zers who are using dating apps as a primary way to meet others. Forty-eight percent of eighteen-to twenty-nine-year-olds say they have used a dating site or app before, according to Pew Research.[5] Additionally, the research found that LGBTQIA+ adults were roughly twice as likely as straight adults to have used a dating platform.

Clearly, couples are increasingly meeting online. At times, it seems as if the idea of a meet-cute or meeting someone at a coffee shop or bar is inconceivable. Romantic comedies shaped our hopes for how we would meet someone, but the world is changing. How quickly the old-fashioned way of meeting someone has turned into an expectation of swiping right on a profile.

Part of what makes dating apps so appealing is the access to opportunities to meet someone. Rylee said, "I love the idea of meeting someone organically, but I also realize I don't go out much, so I don't know 'where' I'd meet someone. At a grocery store in the pasta aisle? As much as I want to lean on fate, I also think it's our responsibility to help create the reality we want," she said. "For now, I'm happy being single. But when that gets uncomfortable, I'll consider joining an app."

Dating apps provide an additional way to meet those outside of your social network. In the midst of busy work schedules, it can be a challenge to find time to meet people. By building a profile and approaching dating with intentionality, you can choose to take an active role in your dating life.

Dating app usage surged during the COVID-19 pandemic as lockdowns, social distancing, and limited gatherings resulted in a particularly unique challenge for single adults. The hope or possibility of meeting someone felt grim. The pandemic sparked fears and a sense of loss for how dating, like the rest of our lives, was put on hold. During this time, many individuals considered their need for meaningful relationships and considered how they could become more intentional with their dating life. The typical avenues of how to meet someone were taken away, and dating apps presented an opportunity to meet people.

Like many others, slowing down and being forced to look at my life differently required me to be honest with myself and my desire for a relationship. The year of attending sixteen weddings led me to admit the desire, but the pandemic led me to take action about it.

I realized that if I wanted a relationship, I could become more proactive. Once the ways I would normally have hoped to meet someone were removed, I was able to look at dating apps with a new perspective. As I considered joining an app, I dealt with my fears and chose to let go of the uncertainty around it. Even though I had watched plenty of friends try dating apps before, it felt different when it was my turn to evaluate dating apps for myself.

At the time, joining a dating app felt like a last resort. I was afraid that if I tried it and did not meet someone, then I would be single forever. Processing my thoughts with a friend helped me see that those fears were a bit irrational, which built confidence for me to give it a try. I could always delete my profile if it didn't work out. I could always try it again. This would not be my one and only shot at love.

Hesitations and fears acted as hurdles, keeping me from being fully open to dating. Before I put myself out there in an intentional way, it was helpful to work through those thoughts and emotions. A few weeks into the pandemic, I decided to try a dating app for the first time. After years of hearing about the apps or even helping friends craft responses, now it was my turn. I went into it with low expectations, knowing there was a possibility to meet someone, but with the main goal of wanting to practice putting myself out there. Similar to the proactive decisions I began to make in my career, I began to feel empowered as I acknowledged a desire and took action to do something about it.

As I joined the app, I stepped into an unfamiliar environment and experienced a lot of growth from it. Dating in general provides a way to learn more about yourself and what you are looking for in a relationship. Success stories do not have to imply the end result of a relationship or marriage.

"I've learned online dating is fun," Elliot said. "If you remove the heavy expectations of 'finding the one' and see it more as just getting to know people . . . there is not pressure to 'succeed.'" There is value in practicing dating and learning about yourself and what you want in a potential partner.

You certainly face the risk of rejection when you open yourself up to dating. A positive reality of a dating app is how it takes away the uncertainty of whether someone is interested in getting to know you romantically. With people you know, it can be confusing when signals get misread, but a dating app makes it clear from the beginning. The person's intentions are known. Apps do not guarantee an easy dating experience, as rejection still occurs in a multitude of ways, but the apps do provide clarity on whether someone is interested in you in the first place.

For some adults, the sheer act of swiping on and evaluating someone's profile can feel superficial and even uncomfortable. Mike said, "I found that the app was not great at informing me about the person, but rather giving me their picture first, which then made me more judgmental than I would have liked." When the focus is all on characteristics shown from a checkbox list, it is hard not to focus on image.

Kwame considered whether or not the apps were POC friendly. "It's difficult to put into words how/why this is the case," he said. "It's not so much that the apps themselves are racist, but that you realize you don't fit the mold of a 5'9" educated White guy who loves *The Office* (or in some cases country music, or both)."

Swiping profiles can feel like a curated experience. Even building your own profile can feel superficial when you try to encapsulate your personality through a selection of three to five photos and witty captions.

Dating apps have evolved over the years. Depending on what you use the filters for, you can also ensure you view profiles that align with certain values or interests. The profiles allow for more than just pictures, which can be a great way to learn about someone in a lighthearted manner.

"I am a strong advocate of online dating," said Clayton. "I liked that you had a lot of information about their personalities and that you could see what photos people choose to show people of themselves." Clayton found a relationship through online dating and dated his partner for over three years before getting engaged.

There is no guarantee, but there is the potential. In fact, online dating is now the most popular way that couples meet.[6]

Damian married someone he first met on a dating app. Upon meeting, they discovered that they shared mutual friends in common, which became important to them. "I'm very pro dating apps but I have a success story, so I totally get why people get turned off to them if they have been on for a year or more with no luck," he said. "My rebuttal to that is that if you're on an app you have to have a different mindset than typical dating in person."

There are ups and downs to online dating, just as in regular dating, but it can feel discouraging if you put yourself out there in an intentional manner and don't have success. Pew research revealed that many Americans who used a dating site or app in the past year said the experience left them feeling more frustrated (45 percent) than hopeful (28 percent).[7] Respondents from my own surveys used words and phrases such as "Disappointment," "Tried it, hated it," "I have used it before, it's just a waste of time," or "I would call them a necessary evil."

Despite these realities of disappointment, the pandemic has altered the culture of dating. Trends such as talking about serious issues earlier and spending time dating virtually before meeting in-person led to behavioral changes that align more with relationships compared to the hookup culture.[8] The pandemic helped us become more honest with ourselves about what we want and influenced dating culture to focus on more intentionality.

Dating apps do not have to be the only way to find someone to date after college. It may seem like it these days, but people still meet through friends, at work, social gatherings, faith organizations and places of worship, or other traditional ways. It may be rarer compared to previous decades, but it is still a common way to meet others and build relationships.

Dating apps are a useful tool and can be successful in forming romantic relationships. More important, the apps reveal more about ourselves and others as we navigate the world of dating. We can use dating as an opportunity to learn, practice, and grow.

In the end, personal growth is not limited to the context of a romantic relationship. Friendships also teach you about how you respond to conflict, how you handle stress, and how you respond with defense mechanisms.

The best thing we can all do, despite whatever situation we find ourselves in—single, dating, married—is to learn about ourselves and how to grow in relating with others.

## CHAPTER 12

# (RE)BUILDING COMMUNITY

"Ultimately the bond of all
companionship, whether in
marriage or in friendship,
is conversation."

OSCAR WILDE

The twenties are a transient time. Friends change careers, move, date, marry, and have children, all at different times. It is natural to compare, especially when your own life does not mirror what you expected or when your life stage is different from your friends. But the fact is that throughout our twenties and thirties, we and our peers will enter these phases of life in various ways and at different times.

As the average age of marriage continues to increase, young adults will experience many adjustments as they transition from living independently on their own to joining their lives together with someone. It takes work to fully integrate someone else into your life.

Kristi dated Tyler for several years before they married. "I think if you've put the work in on the front end to ensure this person is aligned with you and your lifestyle and you're willing to put the work in continually, you reap the rewards in a big way when joining your lives together."

Many spend several years living on their own with the freedom to set their schedule, plan with flexibility, and focus on what they want. Living with roommates provides opportunities to adapt your life around others, but there is a different availability and freedom that singleness provides.

When you decide to get married or live with your partner, that mindset does not automatically disappear. Reflecting on her first year of marriage, Erin said the biggest adjustment was how her life was not all about her anymore. "You are constantly having to think about someone else and their schedule, needs, wants," she said. "It can be exhausting, and there are days when you want to be selfish and just take care of yourself."

When asked what she would tell her former single self, Erin said, "I would challenge myself to put myself in situations where others' needs are more important than my own to help prepare me for marriage. In marriage, every day, there is someone you need to put before yourself, and I didn't truly understand what that would look like on a daily basis."

Dating provides practice for prioritizing someone else's needs, as well as the space to learn about each other. Since lives are typically separate, dating is often more intentional due to the need to coordinate and schedule plans.

People often anticipate living together with the excitement of having your best friend around you all the time. While time spent with your partner is never truly 24/7, the global pandemic in 2020 changed time together for couples around the world. "A big surprise for me was how easy it is to just coexist," Ashley said. "Especially in this quarantine pandemic, we are in the house together all day, but there are days that we don't intentionally connect."

Matt commented how an adjustment of marriage during the pandemic was being together all the time and sharing a space while working. "Yes, we may spend a lot of time together now, but how much of that is quality?" he said. "Most of it is doing chores together like cooking or cleaning. It was confusing because it felt like we were spending so much time together, but none of it was fun. We had to continue to build fun activities or date nights in order to make sure we were still building and investing in our relationship with quality time."

Pandemic-induced quarantine or not, it can be challenging to be around someone and not take the time together for granted. Date nights and making time for fun and quality time is so important for a marriage, especially once children enter the picture. Similar to investing in other relationships, intentionality is key.

With all of these adjustments, it is clear why dating can be beneficial to learn about your partner and their quirks, strengths, and weak spots. Knowing how you work together as a team will benefit your relationship down the road.

In any life-stage transition, there is a natural feeling of grief for leaving behind the old stage to enter into the new. There is a reality of grieving singleness and the season that it was, not because you wish you were single again but because you acknowledge the changes. In describing the most difficult part of the adjustment to marriage, Evelyn said it was grieving certain aspects of singleness. "It's hard to mesh lives and have to make decisions with another person all of a sudden after being single for most of my life," she said.

"The biggest adjustment has been the additional level of vulnerability that you experience fully living together," said Natalya. "Every emotion, every feeling, every mood is experienced by your spouse in some way or another. Constant communication, expression, and forgiveness is key."

Though marriage is an adjustment, this union is what builds the intimacy and companionship of a true partnership. "I think that, in particular, living together has allowed us to grow as 'partners' in everything." Jackson said. "We have time to talk, cook, relax, and make plans together. I've really been able to be next to her through all stages, good or bad, and I think this has certainly allowed our relationship to grow deeper."

As you grow in placing someone else's needs before your own, it builds a strong foundation. "Seeing the way [my wife] will so often set aside her desires for mine, and the joy I've had from wanting to set aside my desires for hers," said Jarron when asked what was important in his relationship. "This is the first relationship I've had where sacrificing (mostly) is so easy to do and brings me so much joy."

Marriage provides someone who knows you on the deepest level and chooses to love you and build a life with you. Marriage does not, however, provide complete security, because life still has a variety of unknowns. Yet marriage does equip you with a companion to face the trials together. "I think many people want to find a partner who is stable, has a steady job, has their life planned out. But in marriage, you support one another no matter what," Jesse said. "It's likely that one of you may lose your job or face some type of crisis, and you should be there for each other through it."

With marriage providing an aspect of comfort and stability, it can be tempting to idolize that person or even the idea of marriage as the ultimate part of life. Jasmine reflected, "It was a very rude awakening the first few months into our marriage that my spouse cannot be my everything. He has failed me *so* many times, and I have too. It's not fair to put that person on a pedestal."

If we are expecting someone to be perfect, we only set ourselves up for failure and disappointment. The sense of security that comes from a spouse is healthy and good, but it is not the ultimate basis for our worth or stability. People are human and will disappoint one another. Your significant other cannot be everything you need.

Additionally, self-doubts and fears that existed before marriage do not suddenly disappear. Lola described this reality: "The biggest surprise was that you still have insecurities from before . . . and that you can still experience a lot of loneliness in marriage."

It is a myth that only single people feel lonely. Friendships outside of marriage are important. Lacey married the summer after graduating college. "I thought marriage would mean never feeling lonely again. That isn't how it works," she said. "Turns out you also need friends."

During the first year of marriage, there are a lot of dynamics to navigate. Relationships require a lot of effort and other couples can help provide insight, encouragement, and counsel. Anastasia advised, "Make sure you've got some people/mentors you respect that aren't family who you can go to when you run into trouble your first year [of marriage]. Family is biased, and some things are just hard to share, so having some older married confidants is a must."

Cecila first learned the importance of mentorship while dating. "Going to friends or family (who are very biased towards me) for advice while dating is only so effective. A mentor can look more objectively and call you out when you're in the wrong or give grace to a person that needs to grow. They can let you know what's a deal-breaker type of fight or a fight that you need to push through to develop strong conflict-resolution skills." Those mentors supported her as she navigated her relationship as it evolved from dating to marriage.

Loneliness does not limit itself to relationship status. Regardless of whether you are single, dating, or married, we all feel lonely at times. As humans, we crave intimacy, companionship, and feeling known. All types of relationships require effort, especially as we navigate the continual changes in community during these transitional years.

## CHANGE IN CAPACITY

Amidst work and other commitments, it takes intentionality and care to continue investing in both new and old friendships. These relationships all contribute to a greater sense of community. A spouse will rightfully take priority in one's life, but it does not remove the need for other friendships. Community expands beyond a significant other.

"I think our society has failed to clarify that relationships can occur on many different levels (familial, friendships, mentors, romantic relationships, relationship with one's self), and they are all an essential part of who we are and how we see ourselves," said Audrey. "If they are healthy and good, they will allow us to see ourselves in the very best light, and that is a true gift."

We know it takes effort to build community, so how do we maintain it as we pass through different life stages? Similar to what it takes to continue relationships with college friends, it requires effort. For long-distance friends, you may schedule phone calls or plan in-person trips to visit one another. For others, it means setting aside time and being available, whether for a spontaneous call or for a meal.

Many respondents shared tangible ways they maintain friendships, such as planning reunion trips, monthly calls, or scheduling girls' and guys' nights. Even if in different life stages, it is enriching to learn from others who are facing different realities than you. As Jasmine said, "I think it's so important to stay curious about others, especially those in different phases of life."

"Being in different life stages is a benefit so I can learn from people in different stages," said Eden. "No matter what, friendships take investing and maintaining. We always have different things on our plates, which means we have to have grace for others and hope they will have grace for us."

Extending grace towards one another is easier said than done, but we all need it. We cannot expect ourselves or others to be a perfect friend, but it is powerful to have others supporting you in the midst of the ups and downs of life. We live in a society built on self-sufficiency and independence, so asking for help, even when we desperately need it, is a hard thing to do.

Peter admitted, "I've learned how much I rely on myself in most things in life. I try so hard to play Superman in most areas of my life, especially now that I'm married, that I drain myself really quite quickly. And what this is teaching me is that being able to trust others to help me is the only way I'm going to make it through life without being absolutely exhausted."

We are not made to do life on our own. Every human being has a need for connection, community, and intimacy. We may have those needs met in different avenues or contexts, but we each need support and encouragement. The relationships we have in our lives also evolve and change with us.

"I also think it's important to evaluate your friendships and what each offers, and see the unique gifts each friend has," June said. "Some friends are going to be the ones you can be vulnerable with, others are going to be the ones that you have a really good time doing activities with. Learning to appreciate those gifts in each friendship is important as they begin to change and shift as people get married."

As you get older, your circle of friends naturally contracts. Many people who responded to my questionnaire addressed how they invest in fewer relationships but focus on quality over quantity. As you settle more into your career and have different priorities, balancing work, relationships, and other commitments greatly limits your availability, thus forcing you to focus on fewer people.

In your early twenties, social life may consist of a lot of group hangouts, but that quickly decreases in your late twenties and thirties.

Jayla shared her thoughts about how relationships change throughout your twenties. "People are willing to be more open, accepting, and vulnerable, but at the same time they have less time for friends," she said. "Whether it's demands of jobs, family, dating, or personal goals (working out, etc.), I see my best friends less and do fewer social outings in large groups that all know each other."

We can only invest in a certain number of relationships at any given time, which means some friendships are close for a season but may drift away over time. It does not diminish the value they brought in that time, but it may not be a friendship that carries on with regular, ongoing communication.

Friendships also shift as friends get married. Close friends may need space to grieve the changes in relationship and extend grace, especially as the couple initially learns how to adapt into married life.

A decrease in relational capacity can be seen in newlyweds as they transition to their new roles as husband and wife. "The beginning of marriage I can liken to the newborn years—there needs to be a lot, and I mean a lot, of hand holding in the beginning to get that newborn to a more autonomous state," said Peter. "And with our marriage, we needed to spend a lot of time figuring each other out in the early stages, which meant not pouring as much into our other relationships as we necessarily wanted to. Now, spending more time with friends, both together and separately, is more natural for us. And we're incredibly thankful for it."

Time spent together will look different. Your friend now has a spouse to focus on, and their partner should be their top priority.

"Does my husband come first?" asked Mia. "Absolutely. Does that mean I have to abandon my friends? *No!* There is balance here, and I'm still learning."

"Married life means a busy life," Ashley said. "You don't own your time anymore. One thing I've found really helpful is to schedule consistent time with my single friends."

For those who are dating or married, please be intentional with your friends who are single. Never underestimate the impact of inviting your single friends along, reminding them that you value their company whether or not they have a partner. And single friends, do not assume your dating or married friends are not available. Be willing to spend time with them as a couple. It takes intentionality from both sides.

"It's also been helpful to bring friends into my relationship," commented Nicole, "so they feel comfortable hanging out with me and him, which makes the longevity as we transition towards marriage easier."

Personally, I feel very cared for when I am invited to spend time with my friend and his or her partner. While there can be moments here and there of feeling like the third or fifth wheel, overall, I feel gratitude over being included and remaining a part of their lives. Sometimes the most meaningful moments are the small ones, such as being offered a ride or invited over for dinner. In those times, I feel part of a greater community.

We miss something powerful when we separate based on life stages. It can be refreshing for both parties to hear from others' perspectives about current circumstances. We can all learn from one another, even if in different seasons of life.

## NAVIGATING THE SHIFTS

When a friend of mine gets married, I prepare myself for the inevitable change in friendship. My married friend will now have her spouse as her main confidant, supporter, and friend. She will naturally need me less, but my need for her remains the same. While my married friends still want—and desire—time with their friends, my role will not be as integral as it once was prior to their marriage. Because my own relationship status has not changed, I notice the difference even more.

These relational shifts were made evident during the pandemic. While we all need friendships, it was natural for married friends to turn to their partner for comfort and companionship. Meanwhile, single friends often floundered with their sense of community abandoned. Normally, singles could have their relational needs met through seeing others at events. When those gatherings were halted, it revealed the sense of prioritization that a partner provides—and how singleness does not provide that same level of priority.

Marriage cannot meet all of your needs or provide a perfect support system in every moment of every day. What I realized, however, was the lack of priority that exists within singleness. I am very grateful for the friendships in my life, but I have no one relationship to prioritize and no one to prioritize me. While I love the ability to invest widely in friendships as a single woman, I started to crave that sense of depth that a partner provides—someone who cares for you, knows what is going on, and prioritizes you over other relationships.

"I have great married friendships and I learn a lot from those folks, but the thought of a few years down the line and who will be left to understand me and hang with me in singleness is a little scary and isolating sometimes," said Brooklyn.

When two people get married, they exchange vows to forsake all others and make a commitment to one another. Those vows create a shift in the relationship, knowing that their partner is someone they chose to stand by and support, for better or for worse.

While singles may have meaningful community, there is not the same level of commitment. Friendships are more likely to fluctuate based on the changing seasons and circumstances of the individuals. Friendships provide less constant support compared to marriage. As our friends move into married life, our friendships with them inevitably change. This change is often accompanied by a sense of loss and can spark fear for what it means for our future, our community, and even our sense of identity.

Depending on cultural norms and societal expectations, there can be a subtle, or even subconscious, sentiment that singles are less mature than their married counterparts. There can also be an underlying false narrative that adulthood begins only when you are married. As Courtney described it, "I often think of myself (or assume others think of me) as less than because I'm single and haven't yet 'achieved' marriage (or even just being in a relationship)."

As more of my close friends get married and have children, I battle various fears and worries. Will they still find me relatable even if I am not in the same life stage? Will they still seek my advice and share about their lives even if my experiences are different? Even though these worries are not my typical experience so far, these fears increasingly weigh on my mind as I get older and remain single.

Pressures to be in a relationship are obvious when asked directly by close friends and family. "Asking 'Are you dating anyone?' or 'Do you have a boyfriend?' is seemingly innocent," Maya said. "But it makes me feel like I'm not looked at as a whole individual without that."

Watching others move into a different life stage can make us feel insecure about our own reality. "What's wrong with me?" we ask ourselves as it becomes easy to think of every reason why (fill in the blank of "I'm not ___ enough" or "I'm too ___"). When I see marriage happening for friends all around me, I cannot help but wonder why it is not happening, or even if it will ever happen, for me. But then I remember how my identity and worth is not defined by my relationship status. And neither is yours.

"We are all just trying to fit in. Whether that means fit in within our workplace and career field, with a partner, with friends, in this world honestly," Diana said. "I think some people put a lot of pressure on themselves due to societal expectations of what a twenty-something should be doing at this point in their life."

We may know intellectually we should not compare, but it is natural to live from the underlying expectation that we should accomplish these milestones at the same time as our peers.

Weddings are about celebrating a marriage, not celebrating an achievement. Some young adults plan weddings immediately following graduation, while some will not get married in their twenties at all. You may be the first of your close friends to get married, or you may be the last. But life is not a race. When we release ourselves from the arbitrary age expectations we place on ourselves, we can feel a sense of freedom and joy over our own circumstances. To live with gratitude, we have to be careful not to compare our timelines and storylines to those around us.

As I celebrated sixteen of my friends getting married in one year, I also accepted that my relationships were changing with those sixteen friends. I became increasingly aware I would not be living in the same life stage as many of my peers. It felt like everyone was moving forward. Meanwhile I was stuck—or worse, left behind.

"I struggle with comparison and feeling like everyone is steps ahead of me in life. I feel like I've already missed the wave of people getting married, and now I will also miss the wave of kids," Mary said. "I think there is definitely a fear of also being alone. It's natural for friendships to change and evolve as people get married and start to have kids, so what will community look like for me, still being single, but the majority of my friends married and some starting to have kids?"

These transitional years are filled with continual change. Friendships change. Priorities change. People's availability and capacity changes. "I've come to realize I'll probably never be done building community—life is transient and people move/change and that need to build community never stops. It gets harder as I've gotten older—more relationships to keep in touch with, less time/margin," Victoria said.

Beyond our twenties, we will adapt to the changes around us and develop new ways to build community. When it feels overwhelming now, we can focus on how we are building habits for how to deal with the inevitable shifts in our community in the future.

The Year of Sixteen Weddings taught me a lot. Though discouraged with the reality of my singleness in comparison to my peers, I also looked forward to supporting and celebrating my friends. I discovered that I could desire marriage and companionship for myself, while at the same time I could feel excitement for my friend who was making that lifetime commitment. One emotion did not have to contradict the other. Giving myself permission to experience both was healthy and enabled me to be aware of my feelings while also expressing genuine joy for my friend who was getting married.

Weddings and other major events are a common trigger of insecurity and comparison. As Monique admitted, "It can be challenging to see wedding photo after proposal photo after photo album of a committed relationship and then look and compare with my current reality. After months of doing that, though, I learned that type of comparison does nothing good for me."

Evaluating each other's timelines may be tempting once the changes start to affect your current relationships. "Comparison is definitely the thief of joy for me," said Katherine. "I moved from the South to a large city after college. In those first few years, my friends in the South were getting married and it didn't bother me. Now, marriage is happening to friends in my current community, and I am constantly comparing myself and how I'm doing to those friends."

It is natural to compare ourselves to our peers, especially when it relates to major life events or milestones such as getting married or having a baby. Instead of shutting ourselves off emotionally, we can learn to acknowledge our feelings while still supporting our friends.

We can hold our desires and live in the present reality simultaneously. Constantly in a state of learning and growing, we can choose to celebrate one another in the midst of our differing seasons, relationships, and experiences.

# PART THREE

# LIVING YOUR OWN STORY

## CHAPTER 13

# THE COMPARISON TRAP

"Nobody wants to show you the
hours and hours of becoming.
They'd rather show the highlight
of what they've become."

ANGELA DUCKWORTH

S omeone once told me they liked my personal brand.
*My personal brand?* I thought. *I didn't know I had one.*

We do not realize what images, ideas, and personas we create when we post, comment, or share anything on social media. "Millennials treat social media as their personal brand—always trying to paint themselves in the best light, surrounded by friends, on an adventure," said Tamara. "It is rarely raw, and almost always thought through, posed, and edited."

Over the years, I have become passionate about being transparent on social media, and I try not to portray a false reality of my life. Inevitably, we all have assumptions based on what we see. For example, when I was laid off, it would have been normal to keep that news to myself and to post on social media as I usually did. I could have overcompensated with my posts so that no one knew about the shocking experience. So that no one knew I was struggling. So that no one thought less of me.

Most of our personal life does not need to be made public, but I believe social media can be a powerful tool to connect, inform, inspire, and encourage. We typically only post positive moments in our lives or highlights of our accomplishments. I chose to post about my layoff because life is hard and messy, and those moments should be talked about as well. Reality does not need to be hidden in the dark.

I will never forget the overflow of comments, calls, Facebook messages, texts, and notes people sent after I posted about my layoff experience. Vulnerability is a powerful thing.

After sharing about the layoff, I met new friends or deepened current relationships because we could understand and empathize with one another about a major life experience. I was often introduced to others when they were laid off because I had been vocal about my experience. I became a go-to contact because friends knew I was approachable and willing to share.

I still receive messages from others who have been laid off or who remembered my story and reread my post. They tell me how helpful it was to know they were not alone. That response is why I wanted to share my story in the first place. That purpose is what fueled this book. While the initial idea for this book was sparked months before, my layoff was the catalyst. What could have stayed merely an idea turned into a mission I had to complete.

Throughout my unemployment, I wrote a handful of blog posts regarding that experience. While those were some of the most challenging months of my life, they were also some of the most influential. Looking back, I am glad that I was open and honest about the realities of job loss and unemployment.

"I really struggle with comparison already, so seeing others post about the best moments in their lives, I begin to question why I am not having the most amazing time with things." Josephine explained she has "made it a point to follow folks on social media who post everything, like you, Cate LeSourd, because it is nice to see that people we think are perfect on social media are human too."

As I shared openly about my emotions, fears, and struggles during this time, my passion to use social media in hard times only deepened. I wanted to help bring to light hidden topics or emotions. That is what led to the praise for my personal brand, explained to me as my willingness to share my failures.

Who would have thought that one of the most shocking, disappointing, and difficult experiences of my life would lead to the development of my personal brand? While I never intentionally asked myself what I wanted my social media to say about me, I realized that people would have assumptions based on what I choose to highlight or promote.

What do others think of you based on what you post or highlight? What is your personal brand? Some respondents admitted they use social media as a way to paint themselves in a particular light; they knowingly contribute to this false reality. "I, too, would post pictures of happy hours and baseball games with friends, but those circumstances were few and far between the tears, loneliness, and heartache I experienced," Tessa confessed. "Those emotions never made it on my social media accounts, because I wanted to portray a fun, young professional who is boldly and bravely living the post-grad life."

We all can feel that pressure or expectation to prove we are enjoying our lives. "I feel like whenever I'm having fun I need to post it on social media so other people know. It's like I am losing out on doing fun just for fun's sake," said Max. "I wonder if that is common with our generation?"

If we do something special or cool, of course we want to post it for others to see. While it isn't bad to want to highlight important experiences, we should take a moment to reflect on our intentions. Are you going out of your way to do something just for Instagram?

Naturally, we want to post an artsy picture of a sunset or show off an image from a beautiful hike we completed. I purposefully take photographs as a way to help trigger my memory, which enables me to look back on enjoyable times with friends. Similarly, many individuals say their social media acts as a catalog of memories. Remember, you can have fun without feeling the need to publicize it.

I am not saying that we should change what we post based only on what others might think. More often than not, the time we spend wondering what people think is wasteful because people probably are not even taking time to think about us. As author Olin Miller first said, "You probably wouldn't worry about what people think of you if you could know how seldom they do."[2] I am saying, however, it can be beneficial to consider how people might make assumptions about your life based on what you post. You are in control over what pictures and status updates you share.

It is naive to think that our social media presence does not reflect on us. Just as companies have social media managers to help shape their brand voice, you are in control of managing your own personal brand. What does your brand say? Based on your social media presence, would people think your life is perfect? Would people scroll through your Instagram and think your life seems flawless? If it is, great. I want to meet you. But if you are like the rest of us, life is hard, and we do not really know what we are doing. We certainly do not highlight those thoughts and emotions on any social media platform.

"Why post about your fears and anxieties when you can post a picture of a beautiful sunset or your engagement ring or your coffee?" Rachel said. "In the moments that I've felt lost and alone during post-grad life, it's easy to wonder if I'm the only one fumbling my way through the real world—and while I know that isn't the case, social media is a powerful tool for making your life seem more perfect than it really is."

"No one ever posts a photo of themselves in a negative setting or negative situation—it rarely happens," Chris said. "It makes you feel like everyone is happy all the time and their lives are perfect, which obviously isn't true."

What we see on social media can foster a false sense of reality, especially when the full picture is lacking. Ada, who pursued a career in music, experienced how social media can be a crutch for friends keeping in touch. "I often felt like my social-media personality was the only one people cared about. Even my closest friends assumed I was great without knowing or thinking to check in with the being herself. I think we're all guilty of that," said Ada. "You just don't realize how real it is until you're the one in need and everyone's operating on assumptions about a person that isn't you."

Life is lived in the daily moments, and our days are usually not full of Instagrammable experiences. It is never the full story.

## THE COMMUNICATION CRUTCH

Social media shapes how we build, invest, and maintain relationships. It influences our sense of connection, which inadvertently impacts friendships. The advances of technology provide access and tools for communication, despite the distance of physical separation. Social media offers great benefits in connecting and staying in touch with major life events, but it only provides a glimpse into someone's life.

"Social media allows people to creep and feel informed," said Heather, "but relationship maintenance is rarely found through this medium . . . Where social media has breadth, it does not have depth."

Social media allows us passive engagement with our community. It is great to see glimpses of the little moments, particularly when not living in the same location, but it might keep us from actively connecting with our loved ones. It is natural to look at what we see and make assumptions about their lives. "Oh, they must be so happy" or "They must love their job." In reality, those assumptions may not be true at all.

"It took a hot second to learn that everyone does some damn good PR for themselves," said Tina. "You don't know if people are actually miserable or loving their lives as much as their social makes it out to be because everyone wants to at least put on the front that they're having the best time in their new lives. Take everything on social media with a grain of salt."

Due to my love of photography, I often post landscape pictures of Chicago on my Instagram. Especially in my first few years living in the city, I often heard, "Looks like you're loving Chicago based on your Instagrams." Yes, I have loved living in the city of Chicago, but that was not the full story.

When I was first laid off, I still posted pictures of Chicago's scenery. If you based your thoughts about me on that, you would assume I was handling the loss well enough. In reality, I cried multiple times a day and felt lost and aimless. Or in my second job—if you looked back on my social media, you would have no idea how much I struggled in that environment because I never shared anything about it publicly. Our lives can be very misleading when viewed from the outside.

"It was also hard to see everyone having these seemingly 'perfect' lives when I was struggling with this big change—but that's our culture nowadays, isn't it? You can paint your life to look however you please on social media, even though it is never the full story," Dakota said. "So many struggle but so few want to admit it. Even though I knew that, it was hard to reassure myself that social media was nothing but the surface of very complicated stories."

Reflecting on his times of struggle and living in New York City, Dan was honest: "Like me living in a living room and questioning what's next, questioning why I moved, questioning who my work is for, attempting to define who my community is, but still managing to post the materials that would lead people to believe I have my life together."

There is always more going on than what we can see. We can seek to understand this before we make assumptions about someone's life or circumstances.

"I think social media impacted my first year out of college by constantly bombarding me with messages and examples of what I could be instead of who I currently am," said Austin. "You'll notice on social media, no one shares the story of the kid who graduated, got a job, seems lost with their life and not really sure what to do next. Instead, all articles/videos/posts are about individuals who are my age or younger starting their own companies, going off and traveling the world because 'What's stopping you?' Social media during college held a bit of inspiration; examples of what I would eventually be and the happiness I could have and share. After college, as time crept by, it became more of a visual of what I could have done and what I'm not doing now. I'm not saying that I couldn't still do that, but now more than ever it seems that the only messages you get are 'Quit your job and do what you want,' but I'm here to say that it's not that simple. It's never that simple. Sorry." Austin said.

There will always be outliers who landed a record deal or started their own company at twenty-four years old but these stories will not help us live our own lives confidently. Inspiring as those examples may be, they set false expectations of what we should be doing. Focusing on those rare examples can also contribute to feelings of inadequacy. We must remember we are still growing and developing as young professionals.

From a different perspective, social media can be an essential and useful resource and platform for a career. Certain fields, such as performing arts, music, and creative industries, depend upon a social media presence. Your image could be vital to your career growth.

As a performer, Gabrielle described how utilizing social media for her career was challenging. "In the performing arts world, your body is your business, and if you are not using social media to gain followers, constantly posting pictures of yourself, posting about shows you are in, posting modeling or personality shots, or posting songs or monologues that you perform, you will fall behind," said Gabrielle. "We are expected to have a following. To have a website. To have a Twitter account. And our followers do matter. And it takes a toll on your spirit because it is hard to separate the person from the product."

You may follow different social media accounts related to your profession. These accounts can act as inspiration and motivation, but we have to be honest with ourselves when they spark comparison or feelings of inadequacy.

Teachers often enjoy posting pictures of their classrooms, but especially for first-year teachers, the images of classrooms can easily lead to comparison. A teacher, Kathryn recalled the pressures and jealousy that would arise when she saw a picture of a friend's classroom. "This is when comparison can start to be tricky, especially on social media, as I realize how much I want to do in my first-year teaching (ranging from activities to classroom set-up to meeting other teachers) but also feeling stressed and stretched too thin," she said. "I thought following teacher accounts on social media would be beneficial, but I actually unfollowed many because it was making me feel like I couldn't measure up or be all I envisioned being my first year."

While Pinterest boards and social media can be a great way to gain ideas for your own classroom, you might be unable to live up to the expectations you have set for yourself, or that you feel from others. This same sense of failed expectations can exist in additional settings, such as planning a wedding, hoping for a promotion, or watching others travel to various countries all over the world. Comparison leads to feelings of inadequacy, jealousy, and discouragement. Social media has a unique power over our emotions and our thoughts, and we cannot ignore its subtle power to influence our perceptions and expectations. These are only snapshots, a glimpse, into someone else's experiences. We must be careful not to compare someone's posted moments with the realities and rhythms of our own daily lives. We each have our own story behind the filter. Behind the hashtag. Behind the post.

## THE DECEPTION

Jobs. Relationships. Travel. Fitness. Beauty. Family. It seems as though there is an unending list of areas in our own lives in which we could compare ourselves and our experiences to others. Thoughts can swirl around, such as *Am I traveling as much as she is?* or *How did he get promoted again?* or *Is my relationship as happy as theirs?* Technology only increases this natural tendency to compare our own lives to theirs.

When asked about the impact of social media, Claire said, "Who didn't get married?! Kidding, of course. But there were so many marriages and pregnancies, it's hard to keep track! Of course, social media just makes it look like so many more."

Scrolling through Facebook or Instagram will highlight these major life moments, whether it is an engagement, wedding, or baby announcement. Other posts, such as someone starting a new job or moving to a new location, naturally make you evaluate your own life and current circumstances.

"I also saw people making these grand life changes—moving across the world for a new and exciting job, being in amazing relationships," said Ryan, "and all I could think was how far away from that I seemed."

I often feel this way about friends getting married and having children. I remember saying to one friend, "I feel like I'm on a train miles behind my friends." My friend responded, "You're not behind. You're just on a different track."

If I focused on how my friends were getting married and dwelled on how I was still single, I would feel discouraged and lonely. If I acknowledged to myself that I felt slightly jealous, I could step outside of my emotions and choose to celebrate their engagements and weddings. That choice leads to genuine happiness and joy in celebrating others, even if you cannot celebrate it for yourself. We are complex humans and can learn to hold conflicting emotions.

"Watching my peers get engaged, accept job offers, move on to different grad schools, and announce their plans for life has made me feel less significant about my plan for my life," Shannon said. "Everything and everyone look better on social media. Heck, my own life looks better on social media! But I have to realize that I can't compare my 'behind the scenes' with other people's 'highlight reel.' I don't get to see their struggle before the engagement or the job offer. But I see mine! It's important to keep these things in perspective before I compare my life to theirs."

Another common object of comparison is how your romantic relationship relates to other couples. "The worst part for me is comparison to other couples who make relationships seem so easy," Myreete said." Relationships take work—and when you see ease, you think you're doing something wrong."

Mikaela said, "I would say the only time I get into the comparison trap is marriage. I do see a lot of couples, husbands specifically, lifting up their spouses in ways that I want mine to do. Of course this is a highlight reel, but I do know some of the couples really mean what they post. It makes me feel like our marriage is so far off from a good one."

Social media offers a glimpse—a captured moment—into someone's life. When a picture is posted, remember there were other moments surrounding that image that are not in an Instagram caption. It is never the whole story.

Megan shared that she will "only follow people where I know the good and bad happening in their lives. It helps me celebrate the good with them rather than see it as a highlight reel." This boundary can help to understand, celebrate, and cheer on a friend when you know the struggles they have faced as well.

Keeping up with friends on social media can paint a false sense of connection, especially if someone is less active but is often included in others' posts. "I find it strange that people who hardly know me can feel like they know me so well," Annie said. "I'm very intentional about what I share with people because it's very meaningful to learn about other people and know their stories."

"We see pictures of friends' lives and think we know what they are up to, when in reality we have no clue how their heart is!" Kaylee said. "I try to create routines of calling my close friends to prevent that from happening, but it is an easy tendency."

While social media is a practical tool for communication, it is not meant to replace other forms of connection. Social media utilizes technology to maintain relationships and helps to keep up with friends and family even if you do not talk regularly.

But the ease of the platform can come at a cost. "I have the biggest love-hate attitude towards social media," Emily shared. "I love following my friends and loved ones and getting a glimpse of their lives now that we are all spread out—it gives us a reason to connect, things to talk about, and brings a sense of connection. The hate side comes from people that take social media as a chance to only show the good of their lives or abuse its power."

Viewing social media as a method to remain connected with your friends can be meaningful. If social media starts to seep into comparison or a measure of what your life should look like, then it can have many negative effects.

"It's definitely tough to see all that others are up to," said Katie. "Are you so incredibly proud of and happy for these people that your heart could burst? Of course! But it sometimes makes me wonder if I'm doing enough, rising fast enough in my field, and putting my degree to good use. Additionally, it sometimes makes me wonder if I'm social enough, traveling enough, and doing enough."

"I would look at everyone's life and would definitely be depressed because it seemed like everyone was having the time of their life post-grad. They had these amazing jobs and immediately made a whole new group of friends but were still able to stay close with their [college] friends," said Mariah. "But then again, it's social media. Everyone posts the best of their life. Even on my own accounts I only ever post the best nights, the best news, and anything that shows how happy I am."

Whether it was moving up to the next grade or receiving our driver's license, we grew up using our peers as a basis of comparison for when we should achieve certain milestones. We have to train our brains to no longer think that way and to accept that our lives will head into various directions. Milestones will be reached at different ages.

If I am feeling down or discouraged and then look on social media, I typically end up feeling worse about myself. When I see someone else get promoted, I struggle with feelings of inadequacy. When I see another engagement, my own life seems so far from that.

Especially in times of transition, we are more prone to compare or feel inferior. Transitions leave us feeling vulnerable. If you are struggling and see pictures of others' successes, it may deepen those insecurities all the more. When we experience change with new people and experiences, we will likely search for ways to feel confident or reassured. Looking at social media is not the best way to do that.

"I think social media is the worst place to be when you are in a new stage of your life because people post what they want you to see. And it's easy to feel like "Oh, why don't I seem sooo happy all the time like these other people," said Serena.

"On social media, it looks like everyone is thriving at their jobs, making tons of friends, and getting fit," said Teresa. "At times it's hard to see past the way we all filter our lives on social media to the truth—we're all just trying to figure it all out the best way that we can, and no one really knows what they're doing. I too often fall into the comparison trap, and that's a dangerous place to be."

Social media is one form of communication, and while powerful, we must limit our use of it or risk being too heavily influenced by it.

## TAKING CONTROL

Many respondents said they limit, or even take a break from, social media, knowing its impact on their mental and emotional well-being, as well as their relationships.

"I actually tried my best to stay off of social media," Zoey explained, "because I was afraid of getting caught in a trap of following friends and feeling like I was missing out on their lives and adventures."

Some recent graduates have limited their use of social media or deleted accounts altogether. "I actually got off almost everything except for Facebook for the year, and I didn't get on Facebook too often." said Sarah. "It felt like this huge weight landed on my chest every time I opened up my newsfeed to see all the people who were in amazing jobs, making great salaries, doing things they loved, getting engaged or married, or traveling. And I was stuck at home, working part time, not sure when my job would ever come through, having awkward online dating encounters, and trying to get healthy (lots of doctors). It was miserable."

Jennifer deleted her social media after college. "I didn't want to see everyone's life updates at that point, nor did I really have any interest in sharing my own struggles with people in the first year and some change out of school. That really worked for me," she admitted.

"It forced me to pick up the phone and call people—actually engage with my friends actively—instead of thinking I knew what was going on with them because of their social media updates."

Setting boundaries by adjusting followers and notification settings can help protect against the effects of social media usage. "A really tactical way I've helped my mental health in regard to social media is deleting apps from my phone (Facebook, Snapchat), removing notifications (Instagram and pretty much any other app), and setting time limits," said Beth.

"I take social media fasts every once in a while. I'll take a month off Instagram every year or so," Catherine explained. "I'm also very selective about the accounts I follow. I'll unfollow people pretty quickly if I find myself having a negative reaction (jealousy, annoyance, frustration) when looking at it."

We can take an active role and set boundaries for ourselves, whether that is time limits, unfollowing accounts, or muting profiles for a time. You do have some control over what you see from who you follow.

For those who work in communications and marketing, you may be responsible for a brand's PR and social strategy. Maddy said, "I think I have a very realistic sense of social media since I've worked in PR four years/been exposed to the back end, so it doesn't faze me as much." With that background, you may be less impacted because you work within the platforms and know their limitations.

Grace commented on how social media inspires her to see how others create and use the platforms. "We've been made so aware of the social media veneer everyone puts forward," she said. "I don't usually find myself believing that other people have perfect lives. We're all working through things that usually don't make it to the social feed."

Remember: No matter what is posted in the feed, there is always much more to the story and the final picture or caption.

As Adrian said, "Just like sports, there is a lot of grinding that occurs behind the scenes of the highlights."

In reviewing hundreds of responses regarding social media, I read time and time again we cannot compare our lives to what we see online. Interestingly, a vast majority know logically we should not compare ourselves to others, yet we often still do. Even if we are aware that social media does not show the full story, we can still be guilty of judging others and ourselves based on what we see.

Some may have strong, negative opinions about the impacts of social media. "It truly is nothing but a filter of one's life, and it breaks my heart to know how much control it has and how much attention is paid to it," said Elena, a social worker. "It is a complete false reality and has detrimental impacts on individuals of all ages."

For my Strategic Communications major in college, I wrote my senior capstone paper on the negative impacts of social media on the development, identity, and mental health of college students and young adults. At the time, there was not as much research as there is today, but it was still clear that social media impacts an individual's confidence and self-worth.

"I stay away from social media," said Peter. "It can be a damning experience, and I personally don't like what it does to people, so I keep my distance."

After *The Social Dilemma* came out on Netflix in 2020, many people who watched the documentary evaluated their notification settings, time spent on social media accounts, or even their social-media presence entirely. Before the documentary was released, some were ahead of the curve. Dominique deleted all her social media accounts years ago. "Best decision I ever, ever made," she said. "I compared myself to everyone, I wasted way too much time, cared way too much about what others thought of me, I had insane FOMO, etc., and honestly, so many of those negative feelings and activities went away or reduced vastly when I deleted my social media."

Even if you do not delete it permanently, you can suspend it for a short period of time. "I have deleted social media many times from my phone to help me stay sane. I do find that I am comparing myself and my body so much more to other Instagram-famous people, which I know is so toxic." Isabella explained, "For me, it's really about balance. I have to make sure I am self-aware of how often I am using social media platforms, and sometimes when I feel addicted, I choose to delete the apps altogether."

One unique impact of social media is on our sense of self, especially in relation to our confidence and body image. It is so nice to have workouts, meal plans, and other resources at our fingertips, but we are now bombarded with images of how to get toned abs or examples of a body transformation, giving us more reasons to feel as though we do not measure up.

"Social media primarily impacts my negative self-talk around my physical body," Nora revealed. "It really comes down to taking a beating on my self-confidence, which turns into envy quickly."

As we age, it is increasingly tempting to compare or hold yourself to certain standards of beauty. Kate said, "I think it's begun to breed a sense of discontent in my body image as my body has changed more and more as the years go on (high-school metabolism is gone!)."

"I compare myself to every single woman on my social media! I am really self-conscious with how others view me on my social media as well," Charlotte bravely admitted. "I want to be perfect all the time, including looking perfect in my photos."

"Unrealistic standards of beauty hit me hard on social media, for sure," said Katherine. "I've found that the best way I can forego the comparison is by setting boundaries with social media."

I struggle with social media just like the next person. After spending time scrolling through different feeds, I can notice a change in emotion or an increase in certain insecurities. While I enjoy seeing what my friends share, sometimes I feel an increase in jealousy over their experiences, image, or even relationship status. As time goes on, I feel sadness over using social media as a crutch to know what is going on in a friend's life.

When something makes me feel off inside, I try to pay attention to those moments and pause. Usually, it is because of something I am dealing with on my own, and I can admit my own jealousy. That self-reflection helps me to accept the differences in our lives and find ways to feel joyful in my own circumstances as well as to celebrate theirs. We can pretend that we are never jealous, but it is a natural tendency of the human heart. Once admitted, those feelings tend to lessen, and I am then able to feel genuinely happy for the person. It does take active effort.

Another way to combat the trap of comparison is with gratitude. When we are presented with images and digital reminders that someone else's life looks a certain way, take time to reflect on what we are grateful for in our own lives. As we practice gratitude, we tend to experience more contentment and joy with our own lives and decisions.

Whenever I compared my résumé to those of my peers, I struggled a lot with feelings of inadequacy. Many of my peers had worked for the same companies since graduation and were rising up in the ranks; meanwhile, I had several job changes under my belt (some forced, some not). These feelings of not measuring up were especially difficult when I worked a minimum-wage job as some of my friends got promoted. Looking at their careers made me feel they were much more accomplished than I.

If I compare myself to others' successes and job security, I set myself up for disappointment. Such comparisons lead me down a negative spiral of self-pity and shame. My career path began differently than a lot of my friends. It took me years to recover from the initial layoff because my career momentum was suddenly cut off. The layoff set me back compared to the peers with whom I graduated. It was a constant battle in my mind not to feel lesser than or behind. I often needed to remind myself my story was different and that I was doing the best I could with unexpected circumstances.

The best way to fight against feelings of inadequacy rooted in comparison was to remind myself of what I could be grateful for: friends, family, close roommates, a church community, and an ability to invest in other areas outside of my job.

If we are not careful, comparison can lead to insecurities and self-image issues. Gratitude can help fight against the debilitating effects, but comparison can seep into our lives whether we realize it or not. Fighting this tendency will be a life-long battle, but we can let it drive us towards greater intentionality in our lives, knowing our own path can look different.

## CHAPTER 14

# DETOURS AND SWITCHBACKS

"You can't connect the dots looking
forward; you can only connect
them looking backward."

STEVE JOBS

omparison happens whether or not we use social media. While social media greatly impacts how we view ourselves in light of our peers and those around us, it is a tendency of human nature to compare and evaluate how we measure up against our peers. This behavior is not unique to any one generation or even life stage. No matter the age, we can always be tempted to compare ourselves, our decisions, and our experiences with something or someone. We are often quick to judge, praise, or question someone else because we are comparing their actions, words, or lives to our own.

You are not immune to comparison, even without digital reminders. You do not have to be on social media to make comparisons with your own life. They are right in front of you. Seeing friends in person can sometimes make it more of a challenge. What do you do when your friend who works at your same company gets promoted before you? Or when your roommate gets engaged before you? Remember that after graduation, we no longer reach the same milestones at the same time as our peers—finding a job, moving to a city, dating, getting married, having children.

At first, the shift in timelines is a lot to adjust to in our post-grad years. We become more aware of our different paths, but our tendency to compare is still a challenge throughout different life stages.

Do you have a long engagement? Or a short engagement?

Do you have kids right away? Do you wait?

Work part time? Full time? Work remotely?

Do you send your kids to private school or public school?

Do you change careers? Go back to school? Start a business?

The list continues on and on. We will not be removed from decisions in our lives that tempt us to compare our own choices with those of others. This goes beyond social media. The desire for social approval and affirmation is strong. It is human nature to want to fit in. We desire to belong while also wanting to pursue what we think is best for ourselves. How do we live in this tension of authenticity and acceptance?

For one person, quitting a job and starting his own business is best for him and his career. For someone else, deciding to stay at the job is best for her. While we can celebrate their choices, we also need to recognize what is best for them may be completely different from what is best for you. As we authentically celebrate others' successes and joys, we can more realistically celebrate our own.

Comparing what others accomplish and experience may directly feed into your assumptions of what your ideal life would look like by a certain age. You may discover that your expectations are not being met in the time or the way that you thought they would be. If you feel that your ideal life and your real life do not match up, you may experience what some call the quarter-life crisis. But do not panic; this adjustment of expectations can help lead to an empowering life pivot. How we choose to face these seasons and challenges prepares us for managing our twenties and the rest of our lives.

## FROM QUARTER-LIFE CRISIS TO LIFE PIVOT

We have all heard of the mid-life crisis: buying sports cars, quitting jobs, and ending marriages. While that may be more stereotypical of someone in their forties, there is a new period of questioning one's direction in life that is happening much earlier—and it's happening to young adults: the quarter-life crisis.

A quarter-life crisis can be defined as "a period of intense soul searching and stress occurring in your mid 20s to early 30s," according to Nathan Gehlert, PhD, a Washington, DC psychologist, who described the person as "highly driven and smart, but struggling because they feel they're not achieving their potential or feeling they're falling behind."[2]

Dr. Oliver Robinson from the University of Greenwich in London found that 86 percent of twentysomethings felt pressure in career, relationships, or their future that could lead to a quarter-life crisis.[3] It typically occurs between the ages of twenty-five and thirty and lasts an average of about two years. According to Dr. Robinson, there are four phases:

Phase 1: defined by feeling "locked in" by your life choices, such as a job, relationship, or both. "It's an illusory sense of being trapped," said Robinson. "You can leave but you feel you can't."

Phase 2: a growing sense that change is possible. "This mental and physical separation from previous commitments leads to all sorts of emotional upheavals. It allows exploration of new possibilities with a closer link to interests, preferences, and sense of self."

Phase 3: a period of trying new experiences and rebuilding your life.

Phase 4: establishing fresh commitments that reflect your new interests, aspirations, and values.

Instead of looking at it as a crisis, perhaps we need to view it more as a catalyst for positive change. Learning to self-evaluate and make thoughtful decisions is an important life skill that is valuable in all seasons of life.

Even if you do not think you are in or will have a quarter-life crisis, you will at some point reevaluate your life, your goals, and your direction. When I turned twenty-five, I had recently quit my toxic job to focus on writing this book. From my story, you will remember that I also worked as a barista for a few months to give myself space to discern the next direction for my career. Whether it was a quarter-life crisis or just a pivotal time for the redirection of my career, I found myself resonating with what someone would go through to resolve these questions. It certainly felt like a crisis at times. I never want to relive it, but I can look back and see the impact those years had on my own growth, both professionally and personally.

In the midst of such a season of questioning, it is easy to feel discouraged, depressed, and numb to what is going around you. You will most likely feel as though you have not reached your potential or that you are falling behind those who are going ahead of you. You may feel as though you are on the wrong career path, in the wrong city, or in a wrong relationship. I urge you to stay away from the pressure of right and wrong decisions. If you are feeling stuck, limited, or hindered in any way, you might be at a pivotal point in your life.

The pressure to make the right decision can overwhelm us, but the only wrong decision we can make is if we do not learn anything from it. In other words, instead of focusing on the term *crisis*, we might be experiencing a life pivot. We can learn to recognize and work through these times in our twenties and thirties. We will most likely experience several major pivots throughout our lives. The confidence and empowerment gained will increase as we move forward. The pressures, angst, and feelings of confusion that occur during these times can paralyze us, or we can use them as a catalyst for change.

I felt numb for longer than I would like to admit. It was difficult to look forward and have hope when I was living in the disappointing reality of the present. While I did compare myself to others, I mostly felt inadequate based on what I had expected of myself. I felt insecure thinking I had not met the expectations I perceived others had of me, but mostly I did not meet my own expectations. I felt like a disappointment. I felt I had already failed professionally at twenty-four years of age.

Part of my internal struggle was my life seemed to keep unfolding in ways that were unexpected or disappointing. A layoff. A time of unemployment. Taking a job because I needed one. A toxic work environment. Those experiences were never in my plan, or vision for my life—especially for all of it to happen before age twenty-five.

If I dwelled on that, I felt depressed. As I mentioned earlier, counseling was vital for me to understand my emotions, expectations, and decisions. Once I did, I was able to grab the reins of my life and make a proactive decision. Instead of letting life keep happening to me, I decided to take action and quit my job. While I am not suggesting you quit your job (it certainly resulted in many tear-filled conversations, anxious moments, and times of fear), it was the best decision for me at the time.

Once I saw that change was possible, I began to allow myself to dream again. I allowed the time of feeling stuck to propel me forward into pursuing a passion of mine: speaking about things that are not talked about, which resulted in this book.

Whatever your life pivot looks like—and I have read countless stories from twentysomethings across the country—I can confirm you are not alone. Periods of self-evaluation are a common experience. And when these life pivots occur, we will later look back and be grateful for the growth that resulted.

A life pivot does not guarantee everything that follows will be easy. In fact, I faced more challenges after I decided to quit my job. However, I remained aware of my emotions and my goals, which helped me continue to adapt as needed. I gained confidence in my decision-making and ultimately ended up with a stronger sense of direction.

Your life pivot may focus on your career, or it could be about a relationship. An end to a relationship or a broken engagement might have left you uncertain about the rest of your life. The breakup could be a catalyst to move you (physically or not) into a different place that you never would have experienced if you had remained with that person.

Your life pivot could even focus on the sense of home. You may have moved across the country or world and struggled to make a home there. While it was a fun adventure at first, it may not be where you want to live permanently. Without the disappointment, you would never have moved back closer to home or to an entirely different place.

You may have already had your first major life pivot point. You may be in the midst of it now. You may sense it coming. This is okay. It is a normal part of life to reevaluate. Sometimes the events of our lives force us to take the time to reflect. We can remain bogged down by the disappointments, insecurities, and emotions, or we can break free from it all and enter into something that aligns more with our authentic selves.

"I think people like to paint your twenties as this glorious time of positive self-discovery where you live in an artsy well-furnished apartment and have fun at happy hours and do well at work and eventually *things fall into place*," Cassie said. "In reality, your twenties are the most challenging years—full of constant self-doubt and comparison and anxiety."

People often reflect on their twenties with fond memories—and we *will* look back on these years and see how we have grown—but it is a tumultuous time when you are in the midst of it. In young adulthood, you will likely experience a job change, an unexpected end to a relationship or friendship, a new work environment or city, or maybe even all of the above. It can be tempting to think you are alone in your experiences. Remember, we are each living our own story and fighting our own individual battles of self-doubt and uncertainty. You are not the only one.

## CHAPTER 15

# SOLITUDE

"Happiness can be found in
the darkest of times, if one only
remembers to turn on the light."

ALBUS DUMBLEDORE

When I moved to Chicago after graduation, I was essentially start-ing over. I left a college campus where I felt known to enter the third-largest city in the United States, known by practically no one. Exciting as it was to be in a new place with new people, it was still lonely. I missed having friends who knew me, understood my personality, or even just knew where I was from.

Kathleen moved to New York City with several of her peers from her college. "I think most people are also scared of making new friends and having to 'start over.' I didn't feel that way, though, because of where I moved to," she said. "I had a group of my close friends from school right by my side as I transitioned into the real world. Because of that, I wasn't scared of the social aspect of adult-hood . . . I feel lucky in that way."

Having friends by our side provides a foundation of support, especially in navigating life in a new city. But it certainly does not eliminate loneliness, which is a natural and expected emotion of the years following college. Of course, loneliness can be felt in any stage of life. For many college graduates, however, this might be the first time you feel the depth of that loneliness.

Even though Whitney also moved to New York City with people she knew from college, she experienced insecurities and feelings of loneliness. "For the first time ever in my life, I feel the most alone. I feel afraid and not sure if I made the right decisions, or where I should go next, or what my life holds," she said. "I have always been someone who is very confident in my choices and making the most of where I am, but right now I feel incredibly unsure. Another addition to this loneliness is that I have never been a homesick/missing person, and I miss my friends and my family more than I ever have in my life."

In addition to the loneliness, we are confronted with the reality that others may not be as open to meeting new people. Whether at work in a new job or a new city, it can feel very isolating to be new. "When you enter the real world, you enter alone. It's a hard adjustment because it seems that everyone else's life is already in progress; they have their jobs, their routines, their Happy Hour place, their Happy Hour friends. Very few people are looking to make friends in the same way you are," said Jade. "That first year can be encompassed in one word: lonely."

Other factors, such as questioning a choice in a city or job, can amplify that emotion. When already feeling fragile, the doubt or disappointment is added to the underlying pains of loneliness. As Bari said, "My biggest challenge of post-grad life at first was definitely loneliness. The loneliness was closely followed by dissatisfaction with my new job, which really compounded the depression-laced depths of loneliness."

It can be very lonely living in a new place when many of your friends are in another location together. "I felt like my friends were all concentrated in a handful of cities (Boston, New York, D.C.) and were having the time of their lives without me," said Tom.

When graduates move abroad to participate in a service program, to teach English to speakers of other languages, to work, or to attend graduate school, they experience a whole other level of loneliness. If you live in another country, you start over and, at the same time, try to maintain relationships across different time zones.

Elena moved abroad to participate in the Peace Corps, but most of her friends lived over seven-thousand miles away. "Most live in the same cities, so as they get closer, I feel that I get pushed farther back. I know their lives are moving forward, whereas I feel as if mine is frozen in time," she said. "But I also fear that I'll have changed so much that we won't have points in common anymore. I guess that plays partially into the loneliness aspect as well."

Not being home for the holidays or other important events can be especially difficult, and can exacerbate loneliness and isolation. After graduating college, Jack pursued playing professional basketball in Europe. "The first year overseas, I'm told, is the most challenging. I faced times of loneliness, especially during Christmas being away from family for the first time," he said. "The second most difficult part is being a vagabond. I don't have a consistent place to settle down because I have chosen to pursue playing basketball for these early post-grad years."

After Kendall moved to Australia, she was living a separate life from everyone she knew, which made her feel disconnected. "I feel like I have this whole life and friends and family in the States and then this whole other life in Australia. It's been difficult balancing the two and staying in contact. You feel very isolated living abroad! I miss my friends so much and am very insecure about my relationships with everyone because social media makes you feel like everyone hangs out every day when in reality they don't."

When I was brand new to Chicago, I was constantly introducing myself to strangers, hoping to make friends. I felt lonely when I showed up to events alone and left by myself. I felt lonely when I missed my friends from college. On a college campus, I would run into friends and spontaneously make plans or decide to go somewhere. In a large urban environment, I have to intentionally make plans if I want to see anyone. It takes effort.

The longer I live in Chicago, the more my experience of loneliness changes. As I established a meaningful community with different groups of friends, I felt less lonely in the city. However, as many of those friends are now married, I again feel isolated as large group hangouts have decreased and time with friends is less frequent due to changing priorities.

## LONELY, NOT ALONE

When I needed time to focus on this book, I traveled on solo trips. I took time off work and rid myself of distractions to go on a personal writer's retreat. I was initially curious to see how I, an extrovert, would feel being alone for days at a time, but I was pleasantly surprised to discover I love taking solo trips.

The first trip was to Seattle for three days. I needed a place with good coffee shops to write in, and I chose a city where I would not feel pressure to see anyone. The purpose of the trip was to work on the book, and I needed dedicated time alone.

I let myself explore for a couple hours, but the rest of the trip was focused on rewriting and editing the manuscript. Over three days, I hopped from one coffee shop to the next without speaking to anyone but the baristas.

That trip helped me discover how much I enjoyed stepping away from the routines and rhythms of my life, especially when focused on creativity. The next year, I tested out a week-long trip to Colorado.

The days and nights were filled with editing and revising the manuscript, and I felt in the zone of my creativity, secure in being alone. I took a break from social media so I could focus, proud of the work I was accomplishing, without comparing myself to anyone else.

Since I was in Colorado, I wanted to experience at least one hike, so I rented a car for the day and drove to the trailhead. The summer before, I had gone on a hiking and backpacking trip with friends in Canada, but I had never completed a hike completely by myself.

While I was hiking, what stood out was the freedom to be unaware of anyone else's speed, needs, or conversations. Alone with my thoughts, I hiked at my own pace. I actually found it refreshing not to have to think about anyone else. Especially for an Enneagram 2 ("The Helper" from the nine-part personality assessment), it was liberating to focus on myself.

When I reached the summit of the 13er (a summit above thirteen thousand feet) I was climbing, I experienced a sense of pure joy. I learned the difference between solitude and loneliness. Even though I spent a week by myself, I enjoyed my own company. I was alone with my thoughts while on the hike. I was focused on finalizing the manuscript. I loved drinking coffee every morning on the porch while overlooking a view of the mountains. I felt empowered by being in a creative zone. My week in Colorado led to me feeling energized and in sync with what I was working to accomplish. I did not once feel lonely or insecure by being alone.

A full weekend of plans with friends awaited me in Chicago. Ironically, within twenty-four hours of my return to the city, I felt lonely.

How could I feel isolated by being back with my friends? While at an engagement celebration, a friend mentioned her evening plans consisted of hanging out with another couple, who happened to be my friends too. At that moment, I wondered if I would have been invited if I had a boyfriend. My singleness made me feel not included.

Loneliness was triggered once I began measuring myself against my friends. That moment helped me better understand my own insecurities and how I can be self-aware to understand why I feel a certain emotion. The emotion itself is often the external symptom of something deeper going on internally.

Sometimes I fear that I will be left behind as my friends enter into different life stages of marriage and parenting. In that moment, I let my fear cause me to feel insecure and lonely.

It helps to identify when and why we feel those emotions, because loneliness will follow us throughout our lives. Your husband may travel a lot for work while you are left at home with your newborn. Your friends may assume you are busy because you are in a new relationship. When you move to a new city, you will have to make new friends again.

Loneliness is one of the most commonly felt, yet hardest to talk about, emotions. No one wants to admit being lonely even though it is a common human emotion. Don't let your feelings of loneliness keep you isolated.

## MENTAL HEALTH MATTERS

Especially in times of transition or change, it is important to pay attention to how your mental health is affected. Both the number of changes and the pace at which you are experiencing them will impact you. During these times of transition, you may be more susceptible to stress, anxiety, or other emotions that affect you and your relationships or even your workplace.

Most major life events or milestones, such as first jobs, frequent moves, career shifts, marriage, buying a home, and the start of parenting, occur within a span of ten years. The changes in early adulthood are generally more muted after the ages of thirty to thirty-five.[2] Due to all these changes happening in such a short period of our lives, it is normal to feel a heightened sense of stress and insecurity. As we mature, we learn ways to develop our personal responses to alleviate, or at least lessen, the sense of anxiety we feel.

It may seem counterintuitive, but repeatedly putting yourself in situations that are uncomfortable can often lead to reducing that anxiety. Ivy had a history of anxiety, which often caused her to self-destruct during interviews. "I was so scared my anxiety would ruin my chance of getting a job. However, as I continued interviewing for positions, I started becoming more and more comfortable marketing myself and my skills."

By continuing to confront the anxiety she had about the interview process, her fear lessened. While this type of exposure therapy may not work for all anxieties, it can be a helpful method to combat unease.

The same can be true for meeting new people, such as going to a party or event alone. Those social dynamics can easily provoke anxiety, but the more you put yourself in those situations and challenge your feelings, the more the fear does not have to cripple you.

Have you ever slowed down to focus on your self-talk? How we talk to ourselves (often in how we think about ourselves) is rarely what we would say to a friend. When emotions feel overwhelming, pay attention to what you are saying to yourself, even speaking your thoughts out loud if necessary.

Intuitively, we know stress plays havoc with our mental health. Adjusting habits to combat the effects of stress may diminish its impact, but it is important to invest actively in your mental health. Positive mental health enables you to set goals, work productively, develop meaningful relationships, and contribute to those around you.

Taking care of yourself emotionally and mentally has a domino effect on the other areas of your life. If you are not sleeping well, you may become more irritable. If you are not exercising, you might find you are more sluggish or tired. If you are not setting healthy boundaries at work or in other commitments, you can easily burn out.

Among the ways to help combat these effects of stress are exercise, counseling, spending time with friends, journaling, and participating in creative work. Make time for yourself since this helps create a healthy place to be engaged with your work, commitments, and relationships.

We need to recognize our capacity and learn our limits. Discover ways that help you cope with stress. It will not look the same for everyone, but learn what works for you.

## SEEKING COUNSEL

We are all anxious from time to time, but if the feeling becomes crippling or consistent, it may be time to seek help.

What separates having anxiety from having an anxiety disorder is persistent thoughts or emotions that affect you daily. The National Alliance on Mental Illness notes, "Everyone experiences anxiety. Speaking in front of a group makes most of us anxious, but that motivates us to prepare and do well. Driving in heavy traffic is a common source of anxiety, but it keeps us alert and cautious to better avoid accidents. However, when feelings of intense fear and distress are overwhelming and prevent us from doing everyday things, an anxiety disorder may be the cause."[3]

As we experience the tumultuous nature of the transition into adulthood, we can feel isolated. We are often left on our own to gauge what will improve with time and what could become paralyzing inaction. When feeling overwhelmed, it is common to feel paralysis in decision-making, which can often lead to feeling stuck or unsure of yourself. Often, you cannot "snap out of it."

It could be argued that it is in these years we would benefit most from professional help, and there is no shame in that. Trained counselors help us identify fears, anxieties, and mental or emotional blocks that keep us from living a full life. Professionals can offer techniques to work through those emotions and mindsets. When those fears and anxieties become debilitating, counselors and medical professionals can provide diagnoses and recommendations, including a referral to a doctor who will determine whether or not to prescribe anti-anxiety medication.

The need for counseling may stem from a specific event or major life change, such as when Natasha had a baby. "It's okay if you need medication to help you get through a difficult time. I had bad post-partum anxiety, and the things that worked for me before weren't helping once I was so sleep deprived. Medication helped me to be a better person, wife, mother, and friend during that time."

Counseling or taking time to focus on your mental health may also be helpful in a time of great loss, such as the death of a loved one. "Mental health is the most important journey I have undertaken in the last couple years. It has totally changed my life, and I wouldn't be here without taking care of it," shared Tamera. "I lost my dad a few years ago, and it totally upended my life. I was confronted with everything I had been trying to hide for years. I really had to work through my grief."

Hailey said counseling helped her foster self-compassion: "I frequently tell my therapist that she can be harsher with me, and she says, "Oh, we already put so much pressure on ourselves . . . I think it's best if we try to take some of that pressure off of you."

Conor believed therapy was instrumental in his life, especially in identifying his self-talk. "We build up such narratives in our heads that are based on anxieties, not facts." Counseling helped him understand the stories and thoughts he was telling himself.

"Life is fragile and so is the mind," Ezekiel said. "Insecurity creeps in without you realizing it, and that affects everything from your personal life to your professional one."

"Mental health is very important, as is self-care," Andrea said. "Therapy is incredibly important when you're struggling with anxiety/depression, and it's a platform to release your emotions that you normally hide on a regular basis."

Counseling provides a means to process the transitions we all face in our twenties and provides an objective perspective on your life. Many people in their twenties go to counseling to better understand their family of origin, to deal with loss, or for premarital or marriage counseling.

I was encouraged to see many respondents advocated for the benefits of counseling. They described how counseling "is the best thing I could have done," "doesn't mean you're weak," and "is awesome." Counseling often marked healthy personal growth.

"I am a big fan of counseling," Peter said. "Getting help from a neutral third party is a wonderful way to dive deep within yourself and begin the healing process likely from years of hurt."

Even if you do not have a specific reason or circumstance for therapy, go anyway. Counseling is a form of taking care of and investing in your emotional and mental health.

"I thought counselors were a last resort for emergencies; now I realize they can be part of your support network ongoing, and it's a way to love people in your life, to be responsible about your own past and ongoing tendencies," Jordan said.

"I've gone to therapy for the last few years and have found substantial help with going," Catherine wrote. "It's helped me reexamine my thinking. Just because I think a certain thought doesn't make it true. With that, it's . . . helped me to prioritize my needs instead of constantly seeing my purpose as helping others."

So far, I have sought counseling at two different points in my adulthood, and I plan to seek counseling in the future as I continue throughout various seasons of life.

The first time was after I was laid off from my first job out of college. I wanted to address how the layoff and time of unemployment impacted my view of myself and my future—my ability to dream. I've already shared about the insights I gained during that time, but I want to emphasize the value and perspective that counseling provided. Although I had friends who knew the basics of what was going on, counseling provided a safe and steady environment for me to process the grief of the job loss and how I viewed myself as a result. It was the counselor's role to listen and provide the professional skills to help me process my emotions and thoughts. While friends offered their support, it was neither their responsibility nor within their capacity to do this.

Zoe has been participating in therapy for a few years and highlighted how it provides a safe place for her. She said, "I've noticed how much less I feel the need to vent to others because I get it all out and process it in a healthy way with my therapist."

Mental health is an important aspect of our overall well-being. Just as we need to know what is going on inside and outside of our bodies, we also need to know what is going on inside our minds and hearts. This can lead to self-empowerment and a healthy sense of ownership over our lives, especially when life feels out of control.

Tyler shared, "The punishing uncertainty, crushing disappointment of the job search, depression after my breakup, separating from all the friends I made in college . . . It all hit me hard. But the worst thing of all was the realization that I hadn't truly been in control of my life up to that point . . . I went through therapy for depression, and it led me to major self-realizations. It was incredibly valuable, as I now feel firmly in control of my own life."

Initially, Tessa tried to distract herself from her emotions of sadness and frustration, but after becoming anxious and depressed, she discovered that counseling was a powerful tool to help her sort through the issues that felt overwhelming. "I often asked myself what

I was doing with my life, why I decided to accept a job in sales, when I could retire, etc.," she said. "These emotions became debilitating. I opened up to a friend about my emotional frustration when she told me she was talking to a counselor who gave her coping strategies that drastically improved her quality of life. She encouraged me to consider counseling in hopes that I, too, could experience the life-changing benefits of talking to a counselor firsthand."

Now, Tessa is equipped with tools to think through decisions and with techniques to help ease her anxiety. She views that time as crucial to her own self-discovery, as it helped her move forward in a better direction for her own career and provided a sense of hope for her future. Years later, she earned a master's degree and became a licensed professional counselor herself.

"It's totally normal to struggle with depression and anxiety, especially in your twenties and thirties because we are all trying to figure life out," June said, "Everything is new territory again, and the first time in our lives when things are not necessarily preset for us."

"Counseling is so important for anyone and everyone! Even if you are happy and all is well, talking through goals, experiences, etc., can be very helpful in understanding how we all cope with changes," Brittany said. "It allows us to be better prepared for our own reactions to situations and how to manage them maturely."

You may think you do not need counseling, but it can serve as a healthy checkup and a way to maintain positive mental health. Counseling is becoming more accessible, especially with the increase of telehealth options, and hopefully will only continue to do so. It is highly beneficial to have an objective perspective from someone else to help you examine your life, often reminding you that what you are feeling is *human.*

## QUARANTINE CHRONICLES

We can also be affected by collective, unexpected traumas, such as a worldwide pandemic. The year of 2020 was unprecedented as we watched the entire world respond to the coronavirus. Within days, our lives changed completely.

On March 11, the WHO declared the coronavirus outbreak a pandemic.

On March 12, the NCAA cancelled March Madness. Other leagues postponed their seasons. Companies discussed remote plans. Panicked shoppers raided grocery stores.

On March 13, the president of the United States declared a national emergency. Cities and states enacted lockdowns. Public transit and travel halted. Businesses shut down, and offices closed.

Within days, COVID-19 was no longer something to watch in the news. It became our own living reality. Our routines and rhythms were disrupted. Our social lives and extracurricular commitments were cancelled. Our workplaces and school systems were forced to adapt via technology.

As the weeks turned into months, our plans continued to be cancelled or postponed. My own family had to cancel a funeral planned in April—a heartbreaking development since we could not be together to mourn the loss of a loved one. Elsewhere, wedding plans were postponed or changed, often multiple times, to accommodate different travel and guest restrictions. Brides spent months planning for and years dreaming about their wedding only for the event to change before their eyes. No one was able to participate in life moments such as celebrating birthdays, traveling on a family vacation, or even seeing a friend or relative's newborn baby.

As a result, we experienced collective grief and trauma. Not only did millions lose their jobs, source of income, and financial stability, but we were also all affected emotionally and mentally due to lockdowns, social distancing, and capacity limits. Humans are social beings. Isolation and lack of community take a toll on our emotional well-being.

While remote employment offered flexibility and freedom, the world of work was impacted in how we build and foster relationships with colleagues, managers, and other professionals. We did the best we could to adapt to these changes, but we all most likely experienced an increase in stress, anxiety, fear, and loneliness. The pandemic, especially stricter times of quarantine, forced society to operate differently.

"I frankly have never really struggled with mental health before this 'shelter in place,'" Steven said. "However, things have been rocked, and I've definitely experienced depression and anxiety in a way I haven't before. From this experience, I've learned that it's okay to not be okay."

"I didn't really think much about caring for my own self until recently, especially during the coronavirus," Meredith said. "I can't pour into others if I'm empty. It's so important for me to be open, unplug, and transparent with my village."

With the pandemic, it was like we started running a 5K race only to realize it was actually a marathon. The coping strategies of getting through what we thought would be two weeks of quarantine were completely different from what resulted after over a year of social distancing, masks, and more of life at home.

Our mental health was impacted in new ways. The experience revealed the need for community and meaningful relationships all the more. When our typical fast-paced lives were forced to slow down, I think we all began to realize how much we all need support or guidance. We especially realized the need for contact with our friends and family.

We feared our loved ones contracting the virus, and we often delayed visits for months or implemented mandatory quarantine times in order to feel comfortable together in-person. Many of us knew someone who developed life-threatening symptoms and grappled with the uncertainty of how they would recover. Others dealt with the tremendous grief of losing a loved one due to COVID-19. Good-byes were said via FaceTime. Funerals were cancelled. Gatherings to mourn together were unable to occur.

No matter your own unique experience, our lives were rocked by this event. Each of us were affected by the need for long-term mental and emotional endurance. While we all hope this was a once-in-a lifetime pandemic and will not be repeated, we can move forward knowing how to better take care of ourselves and have compassion on those around us.

## SHOWING UP

Our culture is one that values individualization and independence, but the reality is that we were built for human relationships and con-nections. We may be tempted to navigate this decade in our adult life on our own, but we cannot do it solo. We need a supportive commu-nity around us. We may be prone to self-reliance or self-sufficiency, but I urge you to gather people around you. It is so important to have people in your life who can support, challenge, and encourage you.

Friends and family will need you too. It is difficult to watch someone you love struggle and battle internally. You may feel unsure of how you can truly support him. If you know someone who is struggling with anxiety or depression, my best advice is just show up. Nothing you say or do may dramatically change her thoughts or feelings, but keep speaking truth and encouraging words.

Depressed people tend to shut down and distance themselves from their loved ones. They often view themselves as a burden, so anything that inflames that can cause them to withdraw even fur-ther.[4] Feelings of guilt and shame in a person's current state may push them away more. Do not be discouraged by his behavior—let him know you are there for him no matter what.

As a society, we are quick to try to fix a problem by spouting a cliché to make someone feel better in a time of suffering. But what does it look like to come alongside others in the midst of their darkest time?

For the friend who lost their sibling unexpectedly?

For the friend who broke off an engagement or got divorced?

For the friend who lost their job?

For the friend who lost their mom or dad?

For the friend who had a miscarriage?

There are no magic words that automatically make the situation better. We may feel a bit helpless as a friend, but sometimes we don't need to do or say anything. We just need to show up. Be present. Love through action.

The day after I was laid off, my friend invited me over for dinner. As I shared my initial beliefs about the situation and how I felt, she told me she thought I was in denial and predicted that I would be processing the grief for a while. Oh, she was right. While I had hope for how the situation could be redeemed in the future, those months of unemployment were painful—overwhelming and difficult. And the grief did not stop there. It was compounded when I had a job offer rescinded a year and a half later. When you lose a job, you also lose your security, income, career, and routine. From my experience, it was a shock and source of stress to lose the ability to provide for myself. It took years to recover financially, and it has been a process to rebuild my confidence and minimize the self-doubt that resulted.

During the difficult months, some friends intentionally came alongside me. Others seemed not to know how to step into the mess. We want to know exactly how to help or fix a situation; in reality, there is rarely one simple solution. Especially with grief, what we need most are loved ones willing to sit with us in our pain and thereby remind us we are not alone. Every individual will be different so simply ask what they need.

"It's also okay to depend on people who love you and tell them what would help," Maggie said. "If what I really need is a load of groceries delivered, or a hug, or a Netflix documentary recommendation, or a person to cry to for two hours, it's much easier to say that than make people who love me guess, usually fail, and then not feel better."

With grief, it can be difficult to know how to care for a friend or family member. Sometimes the need is for laughter and joy to give his mind a break from the loss or tragedy. Sometimes the need is to listen actively as she processes her thoughts. Sometimes the need is to show up with a meal or watch a movie together. There is no singular, "right" way to care for someone.

If you are the one grieving or struggling, how do you humbly accept or receive the help that your friends or family are trying to provide? It may seem impossible to try and communicate what you need. Most loved ones want to help; they just do not know how.

"I struggle with anxiety like many others. What has helped me is getting help when I need it and not being afraid to talk to someone," Matt said. "It's also important to be upfront and honest with people close to you. That way they can help you even when you don't want to ask for help or don't know you need it. A strong support system that's in the loop on what you struggle with is important to taking care of yourself when you're unable to."

Receiving help can be especially difficult in a culture that values self-sufficiency. Admitting you need help and support from family and friends requires humility and strength. "It's so important to share our fears and anxious thoughts with close friends—they become so much less powerful when spoken aloud, and community plays a huge role for me in overcoming fear that at times has been crippling," said Odette.

It is natural to feel alone in our circumstances or thoughts and to isolate when we do not feel like there could be anyone else who understands what we are facing. While there will not be someone who fully comprehends your exact situation in your precise time, we miss out on experiencing empathy and grace from one another when we keep our struggles to ourselves. Shame keeps us in the dark. Hiding. Alone.

Conversely, as we speak our fears, insecurities, and emotions out loud, I do believe they can lose power. We allow others to speak life and truth and encouragement. We cannot do it on our own. Community is crucial for that.

## CHAPTER 16

# BOUNDARY LINES

"Boundaries define us. They define
what is me and what is not me.
A boundary shows me where I end
and someone else begins, leading
me to a sense of ownership."

DR. HENRY CLOUD AND DR. JOHN TOWNSEND

With so much of our work involving our mental energy, we can easily burn out. Our mental capacity is limited. By the end of the day or week, we are often so tired that we look for Netflix shows to binge watch so we can forget. We need to take time to recharge. Technology and the internet have changed what most of our jobs require. Previously, we would need to rest our bodies after a long day's work. Now, we need to rest our brains.

Research shows that millennials have the highest rates of depression and anxiety of any previous generation, with job concerns high on their list of worries.[2] With the world becoming more and more digital and automated, Gen Z faces a similar risk. To perform our best at work, we need to take care of ourselves by setting healthy boundaries. No one is going to set them for you. Whether in an office full time or at home, you must set them for yourself.

## OUT OF OFFICE

Many respondents mentioned that one of the greatest challenges they faced in the workplace is setting boundaries and establishing work-life balance for their own lives.

Wesley, a practicing lawyer, described how work-life balance is a common struggle in professional settings. "It is difficult to know when to call it quits for a day and head home," he said. "I can't say I have the perfect answer for how to fix this, but what I have learned is that you need to set boundaries for yourself. You sign up for groups or clubs to make sure you are leaving the office, and you make sure all your coworkers know what these activities are so that they can be aware of your timing."

Hadley needed to set boundaries when everyone was working seventy to eighty hours a week during tax season. "You just have to remember that work is not everything and really have to figure out what you value and what you want your life to look like in the future," she said. "If you establish yourself as the workaholic from the beginning, it's hard to step back from that—having boundaries is key."

The tendency to overwork can be common especially when trying to prove a strong work ethic or establish one's credibility. "Work-life boundaries are very difficult for me, mostly due to my nature to want to please my managers/teams and to produce above-and-beyond work even if unrealistic," said Taylor.

"Work will be all consuming if you don't set boundaries," Kyle said.

Work-life balance does not come automatically; it takes time and effort. For most, establishing boundaries involves trial and error. It can be as simple as taking a vacation (seriously, do it), taking a sick day when we are indeed sick, or establishing boundaries for when and how often we respond to emails.

Recently diagnosed with anxiety, Brianna discovered how much it weighed her down day-to-day. "This stemmed from a stressful job in the event industry, with long hours and never feeling as though the effort I put in was enough to progress my career forward. From this, I realized how important it is to set boundaries and know when to step back, take breaks, and keep mental health stable."

Beth noticed her declines in mental health often correlate with working too many hours at her large advertising agency. "I don't get adequate sleep, I don't prioritize meal prepping and going to the gym, which causes my body to lack energy and proper nutrition," she said. "My digestion really suffers, and I stay in 'fight or flight' much more than 'rest and digest.'"

No one is going to teach you how to have a healthy work-life balance. Rarely do I ever hear, "Hey, Cate, you've been working a lot lately. You should take a break." Companies and employers expect peak work performance and will not object if we go above and beyond. Obviously, we ought to give our best efforts on the job. At the same time, we need to be mindful of our limits to perform our best work.

From the minute I started my first job out of college, I was passionate to find a work-life balance. The first boundary I tried to keep was leaving my computer at the office unless I absolutely had to do work after hours for a deadline. I preferred to stay late at the office physically, rather than bring work home, to protect that sense of home life.

I was surprised at how easy it is to break those boundaries. In new work situations, I tend to overexert myself, hoping to prove they made the right hire. Hard work is important, but working for the sake of working becomes problematic.

When I got into the habit of working in the late evenings, my attitude toward work shifted. As I began to feel burned out, I consciously refreshed and reset my boundaries.

Another common threat to work-life balance occurs when we start a new job. Because we are trying to build relationships, trust, and respect, it can be tempting to overexert ourselves to establish credibility. With work tied to performance, there will naturally be an element of feeling pressure to showcase your talent and effort. However, there is a difference in demonstrating it versus proving it.

"When you're starting off in your career, there's pressure to prove yourself, bust your butt, establish a positive reputation as a hard worker and go-getter. Which, don't get me wrong, is a good thing to do," said Skyler. "But I've had trouble figuring out when to turn that off. When are we finally able to sit back and say, okay, I've set the groundwork, and now I can work how I normally do?" It is far too easy to become stuck in that cycle.

Tina said her greatest challenge was, "Learning how to say no. When you start off in a job, you'll say yes to everything because you want to make a good impression. A manager gave me some great advice—be careful who you become in your work life because that will shape who you are in your personal life. If you're constantly the person who gets in before everyone else and stays late, people are going to expect you to be responsive at ungodly hours. The best thing you can do early on is set your own limits for work and stick to it."

Of course, work-life balance has been challenged in unprecedented ways as a result of COVID-19. Many organizations had to quickly begin working remotely full time. With "shelter in place" and our home as our office, any boundaries between work and home life completely vanished.

"A challenge that I've been dealing with for a while is how much time and energy is devoted to trying to prove to coworkers/my boss how much I'm working," Layla said. "There seems to be more of an emphasis on how quickly or slowly someone responds to a g-chat . . ."

The pandemic season will leave long-term impacts on the working world. From extending work from home plans to offering hybrid work arrangements, companies have and will continue to adapt. How do you possibly set healthy boundaries when your work and home life completely intersect?

I am no expert by any means. At the beginning, I tried to keep my hours of working nine to six, but some days required longer hours. While I was trying to protect my evenings, I soon adopted a more flexible schedule, especially since all my social plans and events were now non-existent. A call at 8:00 p.m. to edit a newsletter meant I could take a 2:00 p.m. coffee break.

COVID-19 also brought a separation of employees into two broad categories: nonessential and those deemed essential, especially those in the medical and front-line professions. Due to required in-person shifts, the high levels of dangerous work conditions, or the enormity of the task of their job function, many essential workers found it impossible to maintain anything remotely resembling work-life balance.

As a social worker, Luna struggled emotionally to leave her crisis cases at the office. "Sometimes it feels like the weight of the world is on my shoulders, especially during this pandemic. And so many people are struggling emotionally," she said. "My other biggest challenge has been that none of my good friends are in this field of crisis mental health work, so it's really difficult to relate to my friends who do completely different jobs or are in different fields."

Even before the pandemic, work-life boundaries were vital for a sustainable career in healthcare. As a nurse practitioner, Erin emphasized how her job creates a high-stress environment as she deals with those who are sick. "Since my first ED [Emergency Department] job, I had to start creating boundaries, so I did not take my work home with me. It was hard to build those muscles as I often carried home the emotion, physical exhaustion, but found it was not healthy for me to do that," she said. "It took me about a year to be able to compartmentalize my work vs. home life."

When learning to set healthy boundaries, we also strengthen our ability to advocate for ourselves in the workplace. We learn how to express what we need and communicate how a work-life balance enables us to fulfill our job commitments and produce quality work. After all, we don't want to burn out.

"I've really grown in my ability to set clear boundaries and tell my boss directly when the workload is unmanageable. I usually pride myself on just getting things done and staying on top of my work. But what that can turn into is your boss keeps piling on the tasks expecting you to handle it," Catherine shared. "I've learned that telling my boss that I can't do something doesn't make me weak but instead makes me a better worker because the pushback is necessary to survive."

If you want to change roles or adjust responsibilities, no one will intuitively know to ask if you would fit better in a different role. You will have to work hard, communicate, and try to navigate that opportunity on your own. If you don't want to work in the evenings, no one is going to tell you to stop working. You will have to learn when to put your computer down and realize that although there will always be tasks to complete, it can wait until later.

Advocating for yourself helps when you have the support of leadership and mentors. Tatum said, "One way I'm working on managing work-related anxiety is with something my boss recently said to me—'No one else knows what you need. Ask for what you want. If you need help, ask. If you need a day off, ask for it. No one is expecting you to carry it all.' I feel really grateful to have her in my corner and encouraging her subordinates to speak up. And I'm still working on speaking up."

What are ways you can start implementing healthy work-life balances? Be flexible; know yourself and your limits; communicate your own needs and desires; be your own advocate.

## SELF-CARE IS NOT SELFISH

Every time we fly, we are reminded of a classic anecdote about prioritizing self-care. When flight attendants demonstrate a plane's safety features before takeoff, they tell you to put on your own oxygen mask before helping someone else with theirs.

Taking care of ourselves first is vital to our growth and development. It is not selfish to set appropriate boundaries, acknowledge our own needs, and ensure we are operating at a healthy capacity. It is stewardship.

Many respondents reflected on the need to take time for yourself, your hobbies, and passions. To learn how to recharge. To set aside time to ensure you can bring your best self to work and in other areas of your life.

"Take time to invest in you," Lauryn said. "It's exhausting constantly trying to pour out into others. It's okay to take your time and not commit to something right away. Learn to know who you are at your core—your beliefs, your talents, your weaknesses, your insecurities—and move through those."

In any service or human-centered field, you will hear how you must take care of yourself before you can take care of anyone else. When I studied human services in college, we had countless discussions about self-care. As in any endeavor, it is one thing to learn about it in class, but entirely different in practice. Noah, a social worker, said, "It's so essential to find those things and practice them sustainably even if you feel lost/aimless in other ways." Self-care can be grounding when a lot of life can feel uncertain or unknown.

With a Human Services degree, Brooke graduated from college and moved to a city to work with communities in an urban environment. Within five months, she began to experience health problems. With shortness of breath and fatigue, she would pass out. At first, she thought it was heat exhaustion, but when it kept happening, she became increasingly anxious.

"I didn't want to do anything out of my routine. I didn't want to go out to eat. I was constantly in fear that I'd have an episode and I'd faint," Brooke said. "I went to doctors and specialists to have tests done to see what was wrong. I lost about fifteen pounds that summer from the anxiousness. No one ever found anything that was wrong and started to suggest that I take anti-depressants."

Brooke realized this was a wake-up call this for self-care. By not giving herself time to rest, the impact of the stress of working full time and trying to engage full time with the community around her took a physical toll. "I was wrestling with these huge systemic issues like mass incarceration, inherited poverty, widespread addiction, community policing, etc.," she recalled. "Wrestling with these issues is important. However, baby-adult-sheltered me was not going to solve these issues in my first year of adulthood."

After about six months of building new habits and trying to focus on sustainable self-care, the fainting spells eventually stopped, and most of the anxiety subsided. "However, the lesson to find balance really stuck [with me]," Brooke said. "It's something I'm still striving for these days, and something I've learned you have to be really intentional about. There's nothing selfish about learning to say no to things and setting good boundaries for yourself!"

Erin said she goes to counseling regularly to process what she sees as a nurse practitioner and the stress she deals with at work. She also shared a practical tip: "I also take a bath every single night; this is my 'me time.' The twenty minutes in the bath is my time to wash away the day, relax, and let the stress fall away."

Self-care looks different for everyone. It is not always a glass of wine in a bubble bath with dark chocolate (though, that sounds nice, right?). Self-care is individualized and personalized. For me, self-care can be spending time with a friend at a coffee shop or on a walk, going on a long bike ride by myself, or reading a book in my hammock by Lake Michigan. Take time to figure out what recharges you and carve out time intentionally to do that.

When I asked respondents what they do to foster mental health, they answered with recommendations such as therapy, time outside, sleeping well, eating healthy, staying active, massages, journaling, yoga, art, reading, movies, meditation, prayer, listening to music or podcasts, going for walks, alone time, exercise, gratitude, nature, and of course, chocolate. "There is no 'one size fits all' for mental health and self-care, so it's just about trying things and taking note of how it affects you," advised June.

"Being relatively introverted, I enjoy some good alone time," said Peter. "And while I don't get much alone time, I do know that is needed and that need has been communicated within my marriage. If I can get just a couple days a month where I have a little bit of time where I don't need to talk, think about any plans, or really do anything other than what is individually stimulating for me (work on stuff usually) . . . it's a huge help in keeping me even keeled. The biggest hurdle in this for me was realizing that I didn't need to feel bad about telling my wife that I recharge by way of a couple hours a month to just be by myself. When doing this affords me to be a better version of myself, it's actually what I owe my wife."

That is the point of self-care. It is not to participate in a trend. It is to take care of yourself so that you can be a faithful steward of the life you have been given—your greatest resource as you move forward in other seasons of life.

Discovering the habits and methods that help you deal with the emotional upheaval of life's challenges, transitions, and events will only help you in the future.

## CHAPTER 17

# THE SECRET IS OUT

"All human wisdom is contained in
these two words—Wait and hope"

ALEXANDRE DUMAS

The worst of the transition is over. It only becomes easier from here, right? In some ways, yes. What once felt like an insurmountable learning curve is not quite as steep. The rollercoaster of emotions we have experienced thankfully happened for good reason. This tumultuous decade that required so much from us has provided a foundation to help guide us throughout the rest of our lives.

But first, we need to rewind. I find it valuable to reflect on what that first year of adulthood was like and all we have overcome. After all, a lot can happen in a year . . . and a decade.

"I felt lonely, lost, and a little defeated in the first year out of school (while I was in grad school). I felt like I was floundering around, with a lack of direction or purpose," Emily said. "Now, I see that was a great time of self-discovery. I feel more confident, happier, and proud of who I am and where I've ended up (for now)."

Many respondents remarked on the noticeable differences in their lives just a couple of years after that initial transition, whether a change in career, relationship, or living situation. "I feel one hundred times different now than I did in my first year out," reflected Bari. "During my first year I was dominated by frustration with work and extreme loneliness, but now I've hit my groove. I've figured out how to navigate the real world, I've been promoted into my dream job, I've got multiple reunion weekends on the calendar, I'm engaged to the love of my life, and we just bought an amazing home. It's stunning how much has changed in three years."

There are still challenges, but now there is hope. "Being an adult was a one-way ticket. I feel good now being settled in the real world, but that transition was no joke!" Paige said. "The real world is so, so real. Financially, socially, professionally, personally. I did not expect to feel as lost as I felt in the first year of post-grad life, but it definitely gets easier."

Part of what makes the transition easier is the sense of empowerment and personal growth that develops, with an increased self-confidence and belief in your ability to handle unforeseen challenges and difficult decisions.

"I am more confident now in myself than my first year after undergrad," said Silas. "I believe I can take on new experiences and am a more mature person. Whether it be maintaining a budget, saying no to a party to study, or trying to determine what jobs to apply for, I am better able to handle life today than I was two years ago."

Character is developed through trial and suffering. As we handle situations and overcome obstacles, our sense of confidence and ability to make decisions likely increases dramatically. "I feel more self-assured," admitted Rachel. "Living on my own for two years and moving across the country twice has given me a good deal of maturity and a few crash courses in how I handle adult situations like an actual adult."

In work settings, we have built upon a foundation of education and valuable, hands-on experiences. Our professional network has grown. We begin to recognize our unique skill sets and contributions. Confidence comes not only from understanding our skills but also in being able to articulate values and boundaries to colleagues.

"I feel proud of the work I do and of my contribution to my company and the field at large. I feel more secure in my personal relationships—both with other people and myself," said Cassie. "I feel more certain of what I want and like, and what I know isn't for me, and I'm comfortable standing by those things."

"It's a lifetime of difference, in my career especially but in all aspects of my life," shared Jessica. "I'm more confident, probably the most confident I've been in my whole life. I know how to do my job, and I love it. I know who my friends are. I know who I am too. I'm not saying I have it all together, but it's a lifetime of difference from my first year of post-grad."

For you who are college seniors or recent graduates holding this book, do read this with hope: it does get easier. Hang on to that hope. As Martin observed, "I think the more years you spend out of college, the easier it becomes."

Our lives will continue to face challenges and times of uncertainty, because that is the world in which we live. But we will no longer feel the whiplash and isolation of navigating it on our own for the first time. We have learned skills to cope with the changes, manage our emotions, and make thoughtful decisions.

This new discovery can be an exciting time for continued personal growth. "I have gotten engaged to the love of my life, bought our first home together, have a handsome puppy . . . and as a whole, have started to realize what my future may hold," said Kenneth. "It is awesome, and while every day may present a new obstacle or hurdle, it is just another opportunity to mold myself into a better person and grow as an individual."

When we graduate college, most of life involves question marks, and the uncertainty can feel paralyzing. As we move through our twenties and thirties, however, slowly but surely those unanswered questions diminish.

And as we make decisions, we understand we are not locked into those decisions forever. If you move to a city you dislike, you can move again. If you work a job that is not a good fit, you can change jobs. If you later decide you want to change careers or industries, you can work toward entering another one.

For those of us who needed to pursue further education, we will find more clarity over our career direction through hands-on experience in clinicals or internships. "I feel much more confident now," said Owen. "I'm halfway through PT school in the throes of my clinical rotations. I know what I'm doing with my life, and that's a great feeling."

I initially moved to Chicago with two suitcases and a one-way ticket, not knowing how long I would stay in the city. Before I moved, my family took a guess as to how long they expected me to live there. Answers ranged from one year to a few years to a lifetime. My guess would have been similar to what my brother guessed: one year and then I would move somewhere new, wanting a different adventure.

Years later, I am still living in Chicago. I never would have expected to live in one city for almost the entirety of my twenties. As an independent adult, I have built my sense of home here. But while I love living in Chicago, I do not know how long I will live here.

The truth is, I am still figuring it out. Along with everyone else.

## TIMELINES AND QUESTION MARKS

When I was younger, I thought I would be married and in a solid place in my career by the age of twenty-five. In reality, when I turned twenty-five, I was single and I was about to start working at a minimum-wage job. I was more uncertain of my future than ever before. I could not have been further away from where I expected to be at that age. When I compared expectations to my reality, I felt disappointed in myself.

Internal and external pressures can haunt us, especially as we make decisions or see circumstances unfold in a different direction or timing than our expectations. Start to pay attention. Notice how often you say a sentence with the word *should* in it.

At this point, my career *should* look like . . .

My dating life *should not* . . .

By now, I *should* . . .

Our lives are marked with these *should*s. We may not even realize how many expectations we live under until we consciously think about it. Personally, I struggled a lot with this because of how different my initial years after college looked in contrast to what I had envisioned. Compared to my friends, I felt inferior. I felt behind. I felt like a failure.

Even though my career has now recovered, I still struggle when I think about the years that were lost. Were they wasted? At times, I feel an internal pressure to make up for lost time, a weight of performance or a need to please people. And as I already noted, being single when most of my friends have married and are beginning to have children can feel isolating. Naturally, I think my personal life will also never catch up. My friends will move on without me.

I have to remind myself continually to grieve what I had expected and to let go of where I thought I would be at a certain point, professionally or personally. Only then can I see my present realities more clearly and move forward in a healthy, meaningful way. And I can live purposefully in my current circumstances and feel joy over what I do have.

We experience the progressive seasons of our lives—childhood, adolescence, young adulthood, adulthood, marriage, parenting and grandparenting—as they unfold. We assume others know what they are doing, but they are experiencing that season for the first time just as we are. As much as it may seem that twenty-seven-year-old business manager with the good-looking fiancé and golden retriever puppy has a perfect life . . . she does not. It may seem like the thirty-year-old entrepreneur who started his own business after college has it all together, but he does not. We have already addressed the false sense of reality that social media provides, so remember we are all on this journey of life, figuring it out as we go.

Whether at a specific age or not, we often have unspoken expectations for when and how we will reach important milestones or goals. These expectations, both internal and external, will influence us throughout our lives, well beyond our twenties. Instead of comparing ourselves to others or the expectations of society, we need to remember jobs change, people change, ideas change, and ultimately, we change. Or there is a once-in-a lifetime pandemic that upsets all the best laid plans.

We may believe this theoretically but once we embrace this truth, it provides a sense of relief. "I thought everyone had it figured out," said James, "so it was actually kind of refreshing to hear other people didn't have all their plans figured out either!"

Some respondents wish they had been told this truth when they were younger. "I wish someone older and wiser had reassured me that no one knows what the heck they are doing in their twenties (or even after that)," Blaine said. "I am someone who likes to have my life put in order and in my control. Feeling like I was floating out in space with no direction after graduating stressed me out more than I wanted to admit. Having a mentor tell me that would've calmed me down and helped me see clearly."

The uncertainties and unanswered questions about our lives will continue long after our twenties come and go. "Even having a full-time job doesn't mean the self-doubt and comparison goes away," admitted Cassie. "You're constantly wondering whether you're doing this right, or if you should be doing something else instead."

Rachel mentioned being bombarded with the same persistent thoughts: "*What will my next job be? Will I like it? What if I want to leave my next job in two years, just like I wanted to leave my first job? Do I want to get married soon, or have kids?*" She added, "It's become clear that those kinds of fears and giant question marks never really go away. Yes, you gain experience as you get older, and not everything seems as scary as it did when you were on the precipice of entering the real world. But no one has it all figured out . . . and the sooner I realized everybody's just winging it, the more comfortable I was with being uncomfortable."

Beyond this secret—that we are all figuring it out as we go— we also embrace the reality each person moves at his or her own speed. They achieve or accomplish goals at different times, and those goals are likely different from your own. We no longer move in the common trajectory of advancing to the next grade level; we now have our own path to follow to the best of our ability. A friend may finish a master's or doctorate program while you may never want to go back to school. You may have stayed at your company while a former colleague may have left and gone back to school to change occupations. These choices are neither right nor wrong; both involve moving forward in different career directions.

That is part of what makes your twenties so open-ended, and yet, exciting. The pressure or expectation to achieve the exact same goal in four years is gone. You are free to work toward your ambitions based on your individual values, goals, and dreams.

That said, continuing to evaluate your career and life direction may open up new possibilities. "I frequently ask myself, 'What's next?' and have no clear answer," said Lauren. "I have many ideas but do not have a five-year plan. My time working has taught me that there is no linear path. Weekly I consider whether to go to grad school, move to a new city, stay at the same job, or change career paths."

Our lives are filled with subsequent transitions and changes, along with many components that become unknown again as we enter into each new life stage. In those times, it is important to remember that there is no set deadline for our lives. "My future is uncertain, and there are personal goals that I still hope to achieve, but I no longer feel pressured to rush to achieve them by timelines that other persons have used," said Anthony. "I think it has helped me a lot with my current job, which I do enjoy despite the uncertainty."

There is also the continuing uncertainty that comes with marriage, parenting, and other life changes—questions of deciding where to raise a family, what type of schools to educate our children in, and whether or not we will have a dual-income family. With remote and flexible working made available for parents, being able to go back to work is more of a possibility than in our parents' generation. However, that does not mean every individual will decide to work full time after having kids.

"Being a consultant leaves a big question mark if I do have a family one day. I am a few steps away from that at the moment (single), but that is a desire of my heart, and not having a vision of how I could have my current career and my dream of a family at the same time leaves some question marks," Annie said. "Luckily, I am not alone at my company, and there is a group of people looking into a structure that would encourage, support, and promote healthy work-life balance in motherhood."

For women especially, balancing a career with the thought of pregnancy and raising a family can be challenging. "I don't really have a five-year plan, because I will probably have kids by then, and don't know if I will return to work after having kids," Amber said. "My job is not one where I can grow vertically, which I knew coming into it, but I still want to see how I can expand horizontally in my career."

Similarly, try not to be bogged down by a strict plan but instead be open to changing needs that emerge in different seasons. "I'm trying to find the balance of an exciting career that offers work-life balance and possibilities of being an involved mom in a few years. Many career moves involve heavy hours or lots of travel," Laura said. "I'm trying to be comfortable not having a five- or ten-year plan but looking a few years at a time."

Instead of being overwhelmed when uncertainties arise, we learn to become more comfortable in the midst of ambiguity. It is a human response to desire clarity and closure, and I wish I could tell you that life *only* gets better as you get older. But while elements improve with age, the reality is our lives will continue to be filled with unknowns and times of instability. If 2020 taught us anything, it is that so much lies outside of our control.

"At thirty, eight years out of college, I am still trying to figure out what's next," Mary said. "What do I want my future of a career to look like? I'm trying to be kind to myself in this, knowing I don't have to have everything figured out or planned out, but rather look at the situation I am currently in and see if I've become too complacent and if it's time for a change, or for now if I feel okay with where I am at now."

With ongoing decisions, we will have time to discern what is best for our goals, relationships, and values—that is part of being an adult. We can adapt, pivot, and redirect our lives as needed. The goal is for us to learn how to make the best decisions we can with the wisdom and knowledge we have at the time. This not only helps us grow confident in our decision-making but also helps us minimize comparison or judgment.

Zoe emphasized no one knows what they are doing and that everyone is just trying to learn as they go. "I'm not expecting anyone else to be perfect, so what makes me think others expect that of me? When I mess up, I own that I'm human and I made a mistake, and then we can learn from it and move on. Confidence and vulnerability play a big role in that for me."

Of one thing we can be certain and that is uncertainty. Ambiguity does not disappear once you are more settled into your job, relationship, or home environment. The initial decade after college will be filled with life changes, transitions, and new opportunities. We can let ourselves be overwhelmed at every decision that arises, or we can learn how to enjoy the process.

## EMBRACE THE PROCESS

We love sharing that final product. The Instagram post proving we ran a half-marathon but not the hours we spent training. The status update about a new job but not the time we spent searching for the job. The photo collage announcing our engagement but not the ups and downs of the relationship before the ring.

Both millennial and Gen Z generations grew up with technological advancements of the internet, social media, and cell phones. Millennials and Gen Zers desire, even expect, instant gratification.[2] Technology has created this expectation for all generations as we become more accustomed to the way our world continues to innovate.

Hungry? Order food delivery, and a meal will arrive within the hour.

Need a ride? Open the app, and a car will pull up to the curb.

Want to read a book? Purchase it, and it will be downloaded to your device immediately.

The desire for instant gratification may be heightened with younger demographics because we are more accustomed to gaining instantaneous access to almost anything with our phones. However, I think this desire for instant results is part of the human condition. We like easy solutions, quick fixes, and the ability to get the most bang for our buck. We do not like to wait.

This drive and expectation of immediate satisfaction affects the way we view our careers. It takes time to learn about the kind of industry, job, routine, environment, and management style that will allow us to thrive professionally. We cannot expect to know all those answers right away. We cannot skip the process of discovery.

Growing up, we were encouraged, even admonished, to discover our passions and find our dream job. While I did not necessarily expect to have that right after college, I certainly desired to feel like I was headed in that direction. In reality, my career took many twists and turns. Though different from my expectations, I have been given many opportunities to explore different work settings, collaborate with various teams, and develop a broad range of skills.

The concept of a dream job can be misleading when you are faced with the realities of the economy, job market, and business decisions. While we do not have to give up on the idea of working in a dream job or career, it is important to release ourselves from the expectation that we need to be in it right away. I am continually learning how to let go of the idea of having my entire career path determined and instead accept that I am on the journey of discovering it as it unfolds.

"This is not the time to land the dream job," said Austin. "This is the time to discover what the dream job could even be."

You may hold several jobs—even across several industries—before realizing what you want to pursue and what is a good fit for both you and your employer. And that is part of the process. It is equally important to figure out what you do not want to do because it often redirects you toward a new course. What feels like a wrong direction can sometimes be a pivot that helps you move in a better direction.

To grow in our careers, we must learn, make mistakes, develop goals, increase responsibilities, work in various roles, and invest in our own development. We will not become a CEO overnight just as I could not write this book overnight.

We want instant results and success. We know it takes hard work and perseverance, but we are not inclined to admit it also takes patience, discipline, and grit as well.

"The biggest lesson I've learned is to have patience," said Jacqueline. "The patience to wait for my turn at grad school. The patience to wait to move out of my parents' house when I know my whole salary won't be going to rent. And the patience to know that I don't need to be a highly successful adult right now. I just need to be twenty-three."

There is something freeing about that.

What does it look like to embrace being twenty-three? Or twenty-eight? Or thirty-two? Life does not happen all at once—it unfolds. Much of life is lived in the "in between", from one event to another. Learning to appreciate the small moments teaches us how we can intentionally live in each season with all its joys and challenges.

"My biggest fear about entering the 'real world' stemmed from this false notion that doing enough and completing successful work could happen overnight. Obviously, this is not the case," Bryan reflected. "Many people (myself included) have a tendency to think making an impact can happen in the short term and that anything else is deemed a failure. This is very, very wrong. Anything worthwhile takes time and consistent work. You have to fall in love with the process."

Meaningful results require purposeful action. When I decided to run the Chicago marathon, I initially felt hesitant to share on social media that I was training because the fear crept in: *What if I cannot do it?* I was nervous to reveal I was training because I was still in the process of it. I did not know the final result yet and was unsure of my ability to run 26.2 miles.

I decided to post anyway.

Over the course of several months, I trained for the marathon and spent multiple days each week running. I turned down social events to run. I learned how to fuel properly for long runs. I embraced the process. I prepared, and when it came time to try, I finished.

The day after the marathon, friends gathered to celebrate. We were all sore, especially going up stairs, so we mostly sat in an apartment and celebrated the fact that we had all run a marathon. For the amount of time we spent training, however, I could not help but think how it was all over in just one morning. The countless runs over a six-month time period had prepared me for running a few hours on one day. All the time, sweat, and lost toenails had prepared me for one race that was over in a matter of hours.

In February, I had made a bold decision that I would run the Chicago marathon, and I had accomplished the goal that year in October. The marathon was an experience; it was not just an event. I could not wake up and run a marathon one day. I had to prepare.

Similarly, I could not wake up one day and write a book. I knew I had to research the topic, draft the manuscript, edit, revise, and eventually figure out publishing. I had no idea it would take over five years to accomplish. Working on this book required much more perseverance than I ever thought would be required. And at times, it required more than I felt I could give.

Running a marathon was a tangible test of my physical endurance. Writing this book has been a test of my mental and emotional endurance.

The idea was only the beginning. I had no idea what was in store when I began writing, and truthfully, I have no idea what is in store once I publish this book. Throughout this writing journey, I've needed to divert my attention from the end result so I could try to enjoy this time of refinement as a creative individual.

Writing a book while living in the midst of the topic I am writing about has proven a challenge. I am continually learning how to pause and enjoy the process, but the realities of writing and launching a book can be overwhelming. The swirling thoughts of self-doubt can be crippling and paralyzing. Writing about my career failures, traumas, and disappointments can feel extremely vulnerable. I have lost track of the nights I stayed up until 2:00, 3:00 or 4:00 a.m. working on edits and revisions. Even listening to and receiving the constructive criticism and feedback—it is all an important part of the process.

While your goal may not be a book or a marathon, you have probably experienced something like this yourself. You may work extra hours at the office but do not see the benefit yet. You may take on additional responsibilities but still not receive a promotion. You may have a title change but do not receive an additional increase in salary. If you only look at the accomplishments, you will never be satisfied. There is always another promotion to target. There is always more money you could earn. There is always some goal you could strive to achieve.

Accomplishments are valuable as affirmation in a career. Those moments are rightly celebrated because they are meaningful milestones. But if receiving that achievement was the end goal, what happens after we reach it? We will just seek after the next thing. And then the next thing. And the next thing.

"I wish someone had told me to enjoy the journey and the growing pains instead of trying to achieve point B (get married, own a home, find a career, start a family, etc.)," said Desiree. "I think I would have enjoyed each little micro-season instead."

"Keep all things in perspective," advised Melanie. "Just because something isn't happening right now or working out right now doesn't mean it won't come together in the future."

Sometimes our vision can become clouded. Blinders shape our perspective, and we can only see what is right in front of us. The toxic relationship. The unfulfilling job. The discomfort in loneliness. Zooming out reminds us there is so much else we may not be able to see even if all we see is darkness.

I cannot tell you how many times I felt that cloud of darkness during my times of unemployment. Being laid off from my first job at twenty-three years old had not given me much time to build savings. Unemployment checks helped me survive by paying my rent, utilities, and the bare minimum for groceries, but I was left in a high state of stress and survival. Sometimes I wondered if I would ever escape from living paycheck to paycheck. I felt trapped in a cycle of loss and desperation in applying for jobs. It took years to recover what was lost, financially, emotionally, and mentally.

I continue to gain more perspective about those years and the impact they had on me. It does not take away the pain and trauma resulting from those circumstances, but I can now acknowledge the perseverance and resiliency built and character developed.

Times of transition strain our finances. Moving is expensive, especially the additional costs of furnishing a home or apartment. Starting a new job or changing careers often involve classes or programs requiring an investment of time and finances. Marriage results in combining incomes and merging lives into one household. All these challenges are learning opportunities for developing into a stronger, wiser adult.

Challenges or unexpected trials feel like a detour, setback, or wrong turn. In those times, we have to stop hyper-focusing on our own circumstances. Hope comes when we remember that our life is a part of a greater, collective story. We may not always see why or how things happened the way they did at the time, but we can move forward one step at a time, knowing it is not the end of the story.

"Do not despair when things don't happen the way you think they should. You can't see the whole picture," said Amanda. "I don't think anyone can be totally prepared leaving college. Life on earth has a funny way of turning upside down on us and reminding us that we are not in control. You can be equipped, though, [and] have the tools to handle whatever life throws at you."

The transitions that occur within your twenties are filled with overwhelming thoughts and emotions. Karina shared advice she received that helped her: "The years just after you graduate college are going to really, really suck. But they'll also be some of the best years, because later on, you'll see how much you learned, how ridiculous they were, and while you'd never want to experience them again, you'll also never want to trade them for anything!" Karina said this advice "kept me from sinking into depression, that gave me an incredible hope for the future, and kept me from thinking I was alone and/or crazy."

We will not all have the same experiences, but everyone will have times of self-doubt, uncertainty, and unanswered questions about their lives. These years are challenging and at times isolating and paralyzing, but they will provide a deepening of character and personal growth.

"I know no matter how positive or negative my experiences are going to be in the next few years, I think it will add so much to the growth process I am about to go through," Mona said. "I am intrigued to meet the new me in a few years. I am looking forward to feeling differently about things and to eventually be able to make decisions with more certainty as I work towards a clearer goal and life path."

Take time to learn who you are. Understand your values and what goals you have that align with your core desires. As you continue to take steps forward, you can interpret and sift through decisions based on that internal compass.

Especially when you feel overwhelmed, resist becoming paralyzed with fear, inaction, or insecurity. Although those emotions are valid, do not let them stop you from moving forward. Even if it means changing directions and having to take a few steps back, keep moving. One step at a time.

Growth happens in the midst of the process.

## CHAPTER 18

# NOT THE END

"I believe you have the talent to do it.
I believe you have the ability to do it.
Now, you just have to have the courage to do it."

BILL OLIVER (MY POP POP)

Embracing the uncertain process of writing this book has been very challenging in multiple ways. First, writing a book takes a lot of work—much more than I ever anticipated. At times, it felt like an insurmountable feat; I doubted whether I could ever finish it. The manuscript draft was an enormous puzzle of words that needed to be organized in a way that flowed effectively. I worked to combat my own negative self-talk, fears, and feelings of inadequacy. As part of the creative process, I forced myself to reread and edit chapters even when I felt overwhelmed at the task.

Second, writing a book about a current experience or life stage is uniquely difficult. Many times, I had to step back from working on this book because my current circumstances were too much to bear. I had to push through my own experiences to find the words I also desperately wanted and needed to hear.

When I needed motivation, there was a quote that I often thought about that kept me going. It reminded me of my passion for why I was writing in the first place and renewed my excitement for why I must continue forward with the progress: "If there's a book that you want to read, but it hasn't been written yet, then you must write it" (Toni Morrison).[1]

I wanted to read this book when I graduated college. I wanted to read this book more as I navigated life throughout my twenties. I wanted to read this book, so I wrote it. I wrote this book at the beginning of my own journey into the real world and finished as I was nearing the end of my twenties. I wrote this book as I grew into the more adult version of myself. Some chapters were written during my darkest days of unemployment. I revamped and refreshed others when my career felt more stable. All of this book, however, has been a project of love in the midst of living my life.

Chapters were revised based on what occurred as my life progressed. Storylines changed because circumstances in my own life changed. While a lot of the heart and purpose of the book remained the same, there were twists and turns in my own personal and professional life that made me wonder if this book would ever be completed.

I struggled about how the book should end. My life has not ended. My journey has not ended. My career, relationships, and personal growth have not ended.

Additionally, I also wanted to make sure I did not paint a picture that my life has worked out perfectly and now I am all set. First, that is false. Second, this is the lie that I hope this book will debunk. No one has it figured out. I will forever be on this journey and hope to always be a lifelong learner as I grow and experience new chapters of my life.

Earlier, I shared that at the age of twenty-five, I was job searching and applied to over three hundred jobs in a span of a few months. After many setbacks in my early career, that intense period of job searching eventually did change my career trajectory. Once I decided to stay in Chicago, I moved along the process and accepted an offer for a great job at a marketing agency in the city.

Grateful does not begin to describe how I felt. I began my job at the agency and quickly adjusted to the new work environment. I dove right in and immediately had experiences that fostered my career growth, especially by working on an agency rebrand campaign for the first year. The culture was very strong, and I was able to build meaningful relationships with colleagues who became friends. After years of disappointments, I finally enjoyed going into work and was excited to talk about where I worked with my friends and family. For the first time in my career, I felt settled.

After two years, I was ready for a step of growth, especially due to the increased responsibilities I continued to execute. I hoped that would be at that agency because I desired to grow within the company. Although there were some internal shifts within departments at the time, unfortunately, no opportunity appeared.

Just as I began to think about my career growth and how it might need to happen elsewhere, I was recruited for a position at another company in Chicago. I moved through the rounds of interviews, which included building a marketing campaign and presenting it to the team. After I finished those meetings, the company extended an offer to me.

As heartbreaking as it was to think about leaving a culture and job I finally enjoyed, I knew if I wanted to grow in my career (which had felt like an uphill battle for so long), I needed to accept the job offer. That offer provided me with a promotion, an increase in salary, and an opportunity for more ownership.

Even though it was a clear opportunity for career advancement, I wrestled with that decision internally. Due to the setbacks early in my career, I was hesitant. I finally liked my job, so why would I change it? The thought of leaving a position I knew that I enjoyed for an unknown seemed extremely risky to me. How could I give up what I had worked so hard for over the last couple years?

After much deliberation, I took a leap of faith and began this new job in March of 2020, a week before COVID-19 was announced as a global pandemic.

Normally, I would have built rapport with my new colleagues in an office setting. Due to a stay-at-home order, however, I had Zoom video calls as the only way to build connections. I had eight days in the office before we suddenly transitioned into a 100 percent remote environment. By the end of my second week, I was adapting to a new job in a new industry during a global pandemic. Talk about a learning curve.

What I find most interesting, especially about the timing, is how this job provided me with a greater sense of job security than I would have had at my previous position. Unfortunately, there was a major round of layoffs and pay cuts weeks after I left the agency. I am confident I would have been impacted if I had stayed.

A role reversal happened. For the first few years out of college, I was the one who dealt with a job loss, working at a minimum-wage job, a rescinded offer, unemployment, and ongoing interviewing. I watched my friends get raises and promotions while I lived on unemployment benefits and my savings to survive. I felt so alone and isolated during this time, believing most of my peers did not understand what it was like to lose your job and income abruptly.

Now, all of a sudden, I was the one with a secure job. I watched as former colleagues lost employment and had to face the same reality I knew all too well. Even more, I watched as the nation responded to the crisis and unemployment rates dramatically increased around the country. More friends were furloughed or laid off, and it felt all too familiar.

At first, I experienced a heavy dose of survivor's guilt. I recalled so vividly my own job-loss trauma and having my income and career trajectory taken away from me. When I felt triggered or reminded about the pain of my own experiences, I reminded myself that my circumstances were different.

That is what compelled me to finish this book—more individuals would be able to relate to my experience and likely would also feel isolated and alone with their thoughts. I focused time and energy on completing the book so I could finish what I had originally set out to do: help people not feel alone in the ups and downs of life, particularly in the tumultuous time of your twenties and early thirties.

I am grateful for my job and the financial freedom it provided me to rebuild savings and restore a lot of my confidence in myself and my capabilities. I do not know what the future holds, but I have hope borne out of walking through those dark periods and experiencing profound growth.

While I have some confidence in my current job status and the security it has provided, I know that it can be gone in an instant. I never want a job to be the ultimate thing in my life. Jobs come and go, careers can flourish or feel stagnant, salaries can increase or be cut back. I want to enjoy and feel purposeful in my job, but I know it is not the only part of my life that defines me. In the midst of those realities, I highly value my relationships. My passion is caring for others, and that drives everything I do.

Whoever you are, my hope is that in reading this book you feel less alone in your own battles, circumstances, challenges, and joys. I hope you resonated with my own story or the many stories included from others. I know that not every situation will apply to you, but for just one moment, if you felt less alone in this world, I did my job.

For twenty- and thirty-somethings, I hope this book articulates a lot of the emotions you have felt and experiences you have had in these years. I hope it provides a voice into your experiences as you continue to navigate adulthood.

For college seniors and recent graduates, I hope this book will be a catalyst to have conversations among friends and coworkers, allowing for vulnerability and honest chats in what is a hard transition in the lives of young adults.

For college campuses, I hope this book inspires more thoughtful discussions and resources for graduating seniors and that it fosters healthy dialogue amongst students, faculty, and staff.

For businesses, organizations, and places of worship, I hope this book reveals insights and offers intentional ways to incorporate new graduates into the real world and support young adults throughout this decade.

For everyone else, I hope this book provides some insight into the lifelong experience of navigating change and life transitions throughout your own journey. After all, this book contains elements that are simply true of what it means to be human.

# ACKNOWLEDGMENTS

From an initial idea at 2:00 a.m. to you holding this book in your hands today, a lot of time, effort, and emotions went into writing, rewriting, editing, and publishing this manuscript. Many people played an integral role long before this book was ever printed.

Thank you, Mom, for being the first person I told about the idea and for being the first person to believe in it. Thank you for encouraging me to write, challenging me to not give up, and spending countless hours with me reading, reviewing, and editing throughout the process. You were my first line of defense for any doubt, question, or fear I had. Thank you for all the work, seen and unseen, that you did to help an idea become a reality.

Thank you to my dad and my brother, Luke, for also believing in this book, for encouraging me about the creative process, and for helping me see that it was an important topic to write about. Thank you to my extended family who continue to encourage and champion me.

Thank you to my support team of close friends who encouraged me to pursue writing, who received updates when the process turned into years, and who cheered me on when it came time to finish. Thank you for reminding me of the value of this book and for believing in me when I lacked confidence.

Thank you to my groups of friends from Chicago, Elon University, Nashville, Virginia, and other seasons in my life. Thank you to anyone who asked about the book and its progress. While I did not always have an update to share, I am very appreciative of the ways friends showed interest and supported me over the years. I am grateful to have a deep and wide support network of friends all over the country. Thanks for being my community, near and far.

Thank you to the talented individuals who played a critical role in the editing and creative process. Meredith Smith, thank you for your developmental edits; your insightful feedback equipped me with direction on how to make the book shine. One of your comments even inspired the title of the book! Chris Gettel, thank you for your editorial insights and for empowering me with confidence to push forward. Leslie Peterson, thank you for providing detailed line edits, for refining and strengthening the book, and affirming the value of the work itself. Margaret Shannon, thank you for polishing the book at the very end and working your editing magic. Becca Strasburg, thank you for taking my ideas and creating a true work of art for the cover art. Seeing the cover design come to life made the whole process feel real. Larry Taylor, Joe Ragont, and Pat Ragont, thank you all for the tremendous effort to bring this book across the finish line. From art direction to interior design to typesetting, I am grateful for your expertise. Thank you, Rob Tracy, for capturing my personality in my author photos. Bringing a book to publication requires a talented community of professionals, and I am so grateful for each of you.

Thank you to the hundreds of individuals who took the time to write responses about your own experiences. Your willingness to share about your own life contributed toward the depth of vulnerability I hoped to have within these pages. This book could not have been written without the stories, insights, and inspiration I gained from you.

Thank you, dear reader, for choosing to read my words. Every time I became discouraged with writing or the book process in general, I felt compelled to move forward when I imagined you. Thank you for being a source of my inspiration.

Last but not least, I thank the One who gives me the strength to live my story and who gives me the courage to share it.

# APPENDIX

What I find most valuable about this book is how it shares insights and stories from individuals across the nation who were transparent enough to share with me about their own emotions, challenges, and experiences.

I wish everyone could read the responses I received from hundreds of young adults who were willing to share about their lives. This book only highlighted some of the quotes and stories, which offers only a glimpse into the real experiences of young adults navigating their twenties and thirties.

## SELF-REFLECTION QUESTIONS

These self-reflection questions, along with others provided here, assisted the survey respondents in thinking about their own journey into adulthood. Reflecting on these questions at any stage in our lives can be beneficial to our ongoing personal development. Remember, we're always growing.

I would prefer to sit down with you over a cup of coffee and ask you these questions myself to learn about your story. However, I do hope you take some time to reflect on your own, with a friend, or with a trusted counselor. If I were you, I would go somewhere alone (my preference is a local coffee shop) and bring a journal to write down your responses. Here are some questions to ask yourself:

- What has been a highlight from this past year?
- What has been the biggest challenge? How have you overcome it?
- What is something that you are proud of from this past year?
- How would you describe yourself and your strengths?
- What is an area you want to grow in?
- What area of your life is most difficult for you to experience uncertainty?
- What were your initial thoughts when graduating college? What are your thoughts now?
- What have you learned about yourself as you made decisions for yourself?
- What is something you did not expect about the real world?
- What has made you feel the most accomplished as an adult?
- What made you feel most vulnerable in post-grad life?
- What have you learned about yourself through your relationships?
- What do you miss about college? What are you glad is now different?
- What is something you wish you could tell your younger self?
- What would you say to yourself in five years?

## RECOMMENDED READING

Many books are available to provide valuable insights and resources as you navigate your own journey into adulthood. While not an exhaustive list, here are some top recommendations:

- *The Defining Decade* by Dr. Meg Jay—This book is my top "must read" for anyone in their twenties. Dr. Meg Jay compiles learnings from clients as a clinical psychologist and helps twentysomethings understand the importance of the decade and how to make the most of them as we move into our thirties.

- *The Gifts of Imperfection* by Brené Brown—Brené Brown is one of my favorite authors and this book is especially useful as we try to live more authentically. Times of transition can often lead to inaccurate comparisons, paralyzing fear, and self-doubt. This book provides guidance on how to overcome those obstacles and embrace living an imperfect life.

- *Strengths Finder 2.0* by Tom Rath—Personal growth deepens with self-awareness. The CliftonStrengths assessment explains the way you naturally think, feel, and behave. The insights from this book, and additional resources from Gallup, equip you with knowledge and tools to utilize your strengths to maximize your career and life outside of work.

- *Grit: Why Passion and Resilience are the Secrets to Success* by Angela Duckworth—A fascinating read to learn about current psychological research on success. While talent is valuable, Duckworth believes the secret to success is a mix of perseverance and passion. If you do not know how or if you can move forward, believe that you have grit.

A more comprehensive list of recommended books, as well as other resources, is available on my website at www.catelesourd.com.

# NOTES

**Chapter 1**

1. *The Voyage of the Dawn Treader* by CS Lewis © copyright CS Lewis Pte Ltd 1952. Used with permission.

**Chapter 2**

1. Martin Luther King Jr., "Shattered Dreams," in *Strength to Love* (New York: Harper & Row, 1963), 82.

**Chapter 3**

1. r.h. Sin, Tumblr post, 2016, https://rhsin.tumblr.com/post/143849163404/appreciate-this-moment-stop-and-look-around-you.
2. Melanie Hanson, "Percentage of High School Graduates That Go to College," EducationData.Org, last modified July 10, 2021, https://education-data.org/high-school-graduates-who-go-to-college/.
3. Teddy Nykiel, Anna Helhoski, "Alternatives to College: What Are My Options?" Nerd Wallet, October 25, 2019, https://nerdwallet.com/article/loans/student-loans/alternatives-to-college/.
4. Sarah Sipek, "8 alternatives to a 4-year degree," Career Builder, March 22, 2017, https://careerbuilder.com/advice/8-alternatives-to-a-4year-degree/.
5. Suzanne Shaffer, "Alternatives to Traditional College," Collegiate Parent, accessed February 24, 2021, https://www.collegiateparent.com/high-school/alternatives-to-traditional-college/.

**Chapter 4**

1. *The Defining Decade* by Dr. Meg Jay, PhD, copyright © 2013. Reprinted by permission of Twelve, an imprint of Hachette Book Group, Inc.
2. D'Vera Cohn and Jeffrey S. Passel, "A record 64 million Americans live in multigenerational households," Pew Research Center, April 5, 2018, https://pewresearchlorg/fact-tank/2018-04/05/a-record-64-million-americans-live-in-multigenerational-households/.
3. Dan Kopf, "The share of American young adults living with their parents is the highest in 75 years," *Quartz*, April 10, 2018, https://www.qz.com/1248081/the-share-of-americans-age-25-29-living-with-parents-is-the-highest-in-75-years/.
4. Joe Pinsker, "The New Boomerang Kids Could Change American Views of Living at Home," *Atlantic*, July 3, 2020, https://theatlantic.com/family/archive/2020/07/pandemic-young-adults-living-with-parents/613723/.
5. Richard Fry, Jeffrey S. Passel, and D'Vera Cohn, "A majority of young adults in the U.S. live with their parents for the first time since the Great Depression," Pew Research Center, September 4, 2020, https://pewresearch.org/fact-tank/2020/09/04/a-majority-of-young-adults-in-the-u-s-live-with-their-parents-for-the-first-time-since-the-great-depression/.
6. Jung Choi, Jun Zhu, and Laurie Goodman, "Young Adults Living in Parents' Basements: Causes and Consequences," Urban Institute, January 31, 2019,

https://www.urban.org/research/publication/young-adults-living-parents
-basements/view/full_report.

7. Andrew Van Dam, "The unluckiest generation in U.S. history," *Washington Post*, June 5, 2020, https://washingtonpost.com/business/2020/05/27/ millennial-recession-covid/.

8. "Ramsey Solutions," Ramsey Solutions, accessed February 17, 2021, https:// www.ramseysolutions.com/.

9. "Personal Finance for Grads," Investopedia Academy, accessed February 17, 2021, https://academy.investopedia.com/collections/personal-finance -courses/.

10. "Free Budget Template: Easily Track your Finances," Intuit Mint Life, last modified December 8, 2020, https://mint.intuit.com/blog/budgeting/free -budget-template/.

11. Hillary Hoffower, "Meet the average American millennial, who has an $8,000 net worth, is delaying life milestones because of student-loan debt, and still relies on parents for money," *Business Insider*, February 27, 2020, https://businessinsider.com/average-american-millennial-net-worth-student -loan-debt-savings-habits-2019-6/.

12. Brittany Hunter, "Dear Gen Z: Learn from Millennial Mistakes and Say No to Student Loan Debt," Foundation for Economic Education, February 4, 2020, https://fee.org/articles/dear-gen-z-learn-from-millennial-mistakes-and -say-no-to-student-loan-debt/.

13. "2 in 3 Millennials Have Credit Card Debt, More Than Double the Number Who Have Student Loans," Cision PR Newswire, July 25, 2019, https:// prnewswire.com/news-releases/2-in-3-millennials-have-credit-card-debt- more-than-double-the-number-who-have-student-loans-300891044.html/.

14. "Gen Z is racking up card debt after era of tightwad millennials," *American Banker*, January 29, 2020, https://americanbanker.com/articles-gen-z-is- racking-up-card-debt-after-era-of-tightwad-millennials/.

## Chapter 5

1. Maya Angelou, *Letter to My Daughter* (New York: Random House, 2008), xi.

## Chapter 6

1. Helen Adams Keller, *Helen Keller's Journal; 1936-1937* (New York: Double-day, Doran & Company, Inc., 1938), 6.

2. Jay, *The Defining Decade*, xxviii-xxix.

3. Simon Sinek, "How great leaders inspire action," filmed September 16, 2009, in Newcastle, WA, TEDxPuget Sound video, 2:05-3:11, https://www. ted.com/talks/simon_sinek_how_great_leaders_inspire_action/.

## Chapter 7

1. Bill Clinton and Nelson Mandela, "Remarks by President Nelson Mandela at African American Religious Leaders Reception," White House Office of the Press Secretary, September 22, 1998, https://clintonwhitehouse2.archives. gov/WH/New/html/19980923-6565.html/.

2. Van Dam, "The unluckiest generation in U.S. history."

3. Van Dam, "The unluckiest generation in U.S. history."

4. "The State of American Jobs," Pew Research Center, October 6, 2016, https://pewresearch.org/social-trends/2016/10/06/the-state-of-american -jobs/.

5. "Generation Z, the Future Workforce: Trend Brief," Catalyst, February 6, 2020, https://catalyst.org/research/gen-z-future-workforce/.

6. Richard Fry, "Millennials are the largest generation in the U.S. labor force," Pew Research Center, April 11, 2018, https://pewresearch.org/fact-tank /2018/04/11/millennials-largest-generation-us-labor-force/.

7. Marcie Merriman, "Is your business ready for Gen Z?" EY, January 2, 2020, https://ey.com/en_us/digital/generation-z-millennial/.

8. Morley Winograd and Michael Hais, "How Millennials Could Upend Wall Street and Corporate America," Governance Studies at Brookings, May 2014, https://brookings.edu/wp-content/uploads/2016/06/brookings_winogradfi-nal.pdf/.

9. "Gen Z Is Job Hopping: Here's How to Adjust Your Recruiting Strategy," Yello, accessed February 21, 2021, https://yello.co/blog/gen-z-is-job-hopping-heres-how-to-adjust-your-recruiting-strategy/.

10. Howard Thurman in "The Living Wisdom of Howard Thurman: A Visionary for Our Time," (Sounds True, Incorporated, 2010), CD-ROM.

11. Tiffany Mawhinney and Kimberly Betts, "Understanding Generation Z in the workplace," Deloitte, accessed February 25, 2021, https://www2.deloitte. com/us/en/pages/consumer-business/articles/understanding-generation-z-in -the-workplace.html/.

12. Darko Jacimovic, "Stats and Facts about College Graduates Unemployment Rate," What To Become, last modified July 5, 2021, https://whattobecome. com/blog/college-graduates-unemployment-rate/.

13. "The entry-level catch-22," GCF Global, accessed February 26, 2021, https://edu.gcfglobal.org/en/jobapplications/the-entrylevel-catch22/1/.

14. Melanie Hanson, "College Graduation Statistics," EducationData.org, last modified July 10, 2021, https://educationdata.org/number-of-college -graduates/.

15. Melody J. Wilding, "How to Move on When You Didn't Land the Job," The Muse, accessed February 22, 2021, https://themuse.com/advice how-to-move -on-when-you-didnt-land-the-job/.

16. "Recovering from a job rejection," Robert Half Talent Solutions, accessed February 22, 2021, https://www.roberthalf.com.au/career-advice/find-job /job-rejection.

17. "How to deal with rejection in your job search," University of Colorado Boulder, Career Services, July 9, 2020, https://colorado.edu/career/2020/07 /09/how-deal-rejection-your-job-search/.

18. Jonathan Chew, "Why Millennials Would Take a $7,600 Pay Cut for a New Job," Fortune, April 8, 2016, https://fortune.com/2016/04/08/fidelity -millennial-study-career/.

19. "15 Critical Insights into Gen Z, Purpose and the Future of Work," WeSpire, July 2018, https://www.wespire.com/wp-content/uploads/2018/07/We Spire_GenZ-2.pdf.

## Chapter 8

1. Angela Ruth, "Benjamin Franklin – Growth and Progress," *Due*, February 20, 2021, https://due.com/blog/benjamin-franklin-growth-and-progress/.
2. "NCLEX Pass Rates," NCSBN, accessed March 3, 2021, https://ncsbn.org/1237.html/.
3. "Taking the Bar Exam," Harvard Law School, accessed March 3, 2021, https://hls.harvard.edu/dept/dos/taking-the-bar-exam/.
4. Level I CFA® Exam Structure," CFA Institute, accessed March 5, 2021, https://cfainstitute.org/en/programs/cfa/exam/level-i/.
5. Angela Duckworth, *Grit: The Power of Passion and Perseverance* (New York: Scribner Book Company, 2016), 135.

## Chapter 9

1. Excerpt from *Start With Why: How Great Leaders Inspire Everyone to Take Action* by Simon Sinek, copyright © 2009 by Simon Sinek. Used by permission of Portfolio, an imprint of Penguin Publishing Group, a division of Penguin Random House LLC. All rights reserved.
2. Amy Adkins and Brandon Rigoni, "Managers: Millennials Want Feedback, but Won't Ask for It," Gallup, June 2, 2016, https://gallup.com/workplace/236450/managers-millennials-feedback-won-ask.aspx/.
3. "How Millennials Want to Work and Live," Gallup, 2016, https://gallup.com/workplace/238073/millennials-work-live.aspx/.
4. Adam Hickman and Jennifer Robison, "Is Working Remotely Effective? Gallup Research Says Yes," Gallup, January 24, 2020, https://gallup.com/workplace/283985/working-remotely-effective-gallup-research-says-yes.aspx/.
5. Geoffrey James, "Working From Home Makes You Happier and 'Massively' More Productive, According to Science," *Inc.*, July 14, 2017, https://www.inc.com/geoffrey-james/working-from-home-makes-you-happier-less-likely-to.html.

## Chapter 10

1. Excerpt from "Roads Go Ever On" from *The Lord of The Rings* by J.R.R. Tolkien. Copyright © 1954, 1955, 1965, 1966 by J.R.R. Tolkien. Copyright © Renewed 1982, 1983 by Christopher R. Tolkien, Michael H.R. Tolkien, John F.R. Tolkien, and Priscilla M.A.R. Tolkien. Copyright © Renewed 1993, 1994 by Christopher R. Tolkien, John F.R. Tolkien, and Priscilla M.A.R. Tolkien. Reprinted by permission of Mariner Books, an imprint of HarperCollins Publishers. All rights reserved.
2. Amy Adkins and Brandon Rigoni, "Millennials Want Jobs to Be Development Opportunities," Gallup, June 30, 2016, https://gallup.com/workplace/236438/millennials-jobs-development-opportunities.aspx/.
3. Tom Nolan, "The No. 1 Employee Benefit That No One's Talking About," Gallup, accessed August 2017, https://gallup.com/workplace/232955/no-employee-benefit-no-one-talking.aspx/.
4. M. Corey Goldman, "First Time Jobless Claims Rise for First Time Since March," TheStreet, July 23, 2020, https://thestreet.com/investing/jobless-claims-unemployment-benefits-jobs-hiring-economy/.

5. "Employee Turnover in 2020," Bureau of Labor Statistics, US Department of Labor, News Release, September 22, 2020, https://bls.gov/news.release /pdf/jolts.pdf.

6. Carmen Reinicke, "US weekly jobless claims hit 1.4 million, post second straight weekly increase," *Business Insider*, July 30, 2020, https://www.business insider.com/us-jobless-claims-unemployment-insurance-labor-market -filings-recession-coronavirus-2020-7?r=MX&IR=T.

7. Noah Manskar, "US workers file 1.43 million more jobless claims as crisis total tops 54 million," *New York Post*, July 30, 2020, https://nypost.com /2020/07/30/us-jobless-claims-rise-to-1-4m-as-crisis-total-tops-54m/.

8. Zapier Editorial Team, "Misunderstood generations: what Millennials and Gen Z actually think about work," Zapier, January 27, 2020, https://zapier. com/blog/digital-natives-report/.

## Chapter 11

1. Brené Brown, *The Gifts of Imperfection* (Minnesota: Hazelden Publishing, 2010), 26.

2. "Median age at first marriage: 1890 to present," US Census Bureau, accessed August 21, 2020, https://www.census.gov/content/dam/Census/library /visualizations/time-series/demo/families-and-households/ms-2.pdf.

3. "National Spouses Day: January 26, 2021," US Census Bureau, January 26, 2021, https://www.census.gov/newsroom/stories/spouses-day.html.

4. Peter Jacobs, "28% Of People Went To The Same College As Their Spouse", *Business Insider*, October 7, 2013, https://businessinsider.com/28-people -marry-attended-same-college-2013-10/.

5. Emily A. Vogels, "10 facts about Americans and online dating," Pew Research Center, February 6, 2020, https://pewresearch.org/fact-tank/2020/02/06 /10-facts-about-americans-and-online-dating/.

6. Alex Shashkevich, "Meeting online has become the most popular way U.S. couples connect, Stanford sociologist finds," Stanford News, August 21, 2019, https://news.stanford.edu/2019/08/21/online-dating-popular-way-u-s -couples-meet/.

7. Monica Anderson, Emily A. Vogels, and Erica Turner, "The Virtues and Downsides of Online Dating," Pew Research Center, February 6, 2020, https://pewresearch.org/internet/2020/02/06/the-virtues-and-downsides -of-online-dating/.

8. Anna Iovine, "Dating app usage is changing for the better as the pandemic rages on," Mashable, November 11, 2020, https://mashable.com/article /cuffing-season-2020-dating-app-increases-hinge-match/.

## Chapter 12

1. Oscar Wilde, *De Profundis: The Ballad of Reading Gaol and Other Writings* (Hertfordshire, England: Wordsworth Editions Limited, 1999), 13.

## Chapter 13

1. From *GRIT: The Power of Passion and Perseverance* by Angela Duckworth. Copyright © 2016 by Angela Duckworth. Reprinted with the permission of Scribner, a division of Simon & Schuster, Inc. All rights reserved.

2. Olin Miller in "Walter Winchell on Broadway," *Logansport Pharos-Tribune,* January 7, 1937.

**Chapter 14**

1. Steve Jobs, "Stanford University Commencement Address," filmed June 12, 2005, at Stanford University, Stanford, CA, video, 5:06-5:12, https://news.stanford.edu/2005/06/14/jobs-061505/.
2. Varci Vartanian, "Powering Through Your Quarter-Life Crisis," The Muse, accessed August 19, 2019, https://themuse.com/advice/powering-through-your-quarterlife-crisis/.
3. Amelia Hill, "The quarterlife crisis: young, insecure and depressed," *Guardian,* May 5, 2011, https://theguardian.com/society/2011/may/05/quarterlife-crisis-young-insecure-depressed/.

**Chapter 15**

1. *Harry Potter and the Prisoner of Azkaban,* directed by Alfonso Cuarón (2004; Warner Bros. Pictures), DVD.
2. Melissa Dahl, "How Much Can You Really Change After You Turn 30?" The Cut, *New York,* November 24, 2014, https://thecut.com/2014/how-much-can-you-really-change-after-30.html/.
3. "Anxiety Disorders," National Alliance on Mental Illness, accessed August 17, 2017, https://nami.org/About-Mental-Illness/Mental-Health-Conditions/Anxiety-Disorders/.
4. Karen Young, "When Someone You Love Has Depression," *Hey Sigmund,* accessed August 21, 2019, https://heysigmund.com/when-someone-you-love-has-depression/.

**Chapter 16**

1. Taken from *Boundaries* by Henry Cloud and John Townsend Copyright © 1992 by Henry Cloud and John Townsend. Used by permission of Zondervan. www.zondervan.com.
2. Rochaun Meadows-Fernandez, "There's such a thing as post-graduation depression. I know: I had it," *Washington Post,* August 6, 2017, https://www.washingtonpost.com/national/health-science/theres-such-a-thing-as-post-graduation-depression-i-know-i-had-it/2017/08/04/4d163c6a-618d-11e7-a4f7-af34fc1d9d39_story.html.

**Chapter 17**

1. Alexandre Dumas, *The Count of Monte Cristo* (Penguin Classics; Reissue edition, 2003).
2. Skye Schooley, "How to Manage Millennials vs. Gen Z in the Workplace," Business.com, November 17, 2020, https://business.com/articles/managing-millennials-and-gen-z-employees/.

**Chapter 18**

1. Ellen Brown, "Writing is Third Career for Morrison," *Cincinnati Enquirer,* September 27, 1981.

# ABOUT THE AUTHOR

**C**ate LeSourd graduated with honors from Elon University with a degree in Strategic Communications and minors in Human Services and Entrepreneurship. Since moving to Chicago after college, Cate has worked at a venture capital firm, an experiential marketing agency, a media startup, and a PR agency. These diverse work environments have refined her skills in marketing, writing, design, and strategy.

Her first few years in Chicago were filled with intense twists and turns, which fueled her passion for writing authentically and candidly about her own journey into adulthood. She values transparency and its power to bring hope, purpose, and restoration to individuals and communities. Motivated by a desire to help others not to feel alone, Cate wrote this book to bring to light the challenges, joys, and experiences we all face in the transition into adulthood.

Cate enjoys exploring coffee shops, going on long bike rides, and investing in her local community. Keep in touch with her at www.catelesourd.com or follow @catelesourd on social media.

Made in the USA
Columbia, SC
23 March 2022